CW01303575

Kurt Matzler is professor of Strategic Management at the University of Innsbruck, Austria. According to Brightline Initiative he is one of the best strategic thinkers in the world. He is academic director of the Executive MBA program at MCI in Innsbruck and partner of IMP, an international consulting firm, the winner of the hidden champions in consulting in the field of disruption in Germany. His work has been published in leading academic journals. He is co-author of the German edition of the Innovator's dilemma (2011), one of the six most important management books overall (Economist). He is co-author of the book "Digital Disruption" (2016) and "Open Strategy" (MIT Press, 2021), which was shortlisted for the Thinkers50 Strategy Award in 2021, was the best strategy book of 2021 (Strategy+Business Magazine), and is „one of the most important new business books of the new decade" (Gary Hamel). With more than 30,000 citations in Google Scholar, Kurt belongs to the top 20 strategy researchers in Europe and to the top 50 in the world. Kurt Matzler is a passionate cyclist and a solo finisher of the Race Across America 2022. With his participation in RAAM, his team ROTARY RAAMS POLIO has raised more than USD 4,000,000 in donations to eradicate Polio.

ISBN: 9798397250559

Imprint: Independently published

First published in Austria by EGOTH VERLAG as
"Das High Performance Mindset. Race Across America: Was wir vom härtesten Radrennen der Welt lernen können"

Kurt Matzler, Innsbruck 2023

Cover image: Florian Phleps

Kurt Matzler

The High Performance Mindset

Race Across America - What we can learn from the toughest bike race in the world

Contents

Foreword by Christoph Strasser 9

Preface 14

The race of my life 17

My cycling career 21

Race Across America 2016-2019 28

Race Across Italy 37

Race Around Austria 2020 39

The shattered dream 43

Race Around Austria 2021 45

The preparations 48

    Leadership Lesson 1: Discipline - It's easier to hold your principles 100 percent of the time than it is to hold them 98 percent of the time! 58

    Leadership Lesson 2: Use the power of habit 70

    Leadership Lesson 3: Always try in all things to combine what is pleasing to yourself with what is useful to others ... 74

Off to the desert 76

Race Across America 2022 85

The start 85

Day 2 - The big heat 89

Leadership Lesson 4: Be meticulous in planning, but flexible in execution 102

Day 3 - Monument Valley 107

Day 4 - The Rocky Mountains 111

Leadership Lesson 5: Know your why 122

Leadership Lesson 6: Visualize your goal 131

Day 5 - The Great P(l)ains 138

Day 6 - Unbearable pain 145

Day 7 - Sleep deprivation 155

Leadership Lesson 7: Find your individual strategy 163

Day 8 - Saddle pain 169

Leadership Lesson 8: Solve problems while they're small . 174

Day 9 - Motivation 176

Day 10 - The hardest part of RAAM 187

The final sprint 197

Leadership Lesson 9: Marginal gains - the sum of small improvements makes a big difference 208

Leadership Lesson 10: Hire for attitude, train for skills 214

Team Rotary RAAMs Polio - the crew 221

Leadership Lesson 11: Work hard, but plan for sufficient regeneration 227

1.2 million for polio eradication 236

Literature 253

Foreword by Christoph Strasser

It is a great pleasure for me to have the opportunity to write here a few lines. First of all, I would like to congratulate Kurt from the bottom of my heart, he has fulfilled a lifelong dream and successfully completed the RAAM. But what impresses me most is the way he managed to do it together with his team. He has shown what qualities are needed and how important good preparation is. But also what flexibility is needed on the road, because even the best plan rarely holds and must always be adapted on the course.

What does it take for a cyclist to race more than 4800 kilometers and 42,000 meters of climbing in less than twelve days under one's own muscle power on a road bike, enduring brutal heat, bone-chilling cold, whipping thunderstorms and gusty winds? What is more important, body or mind? To these questions, every person who has witnessed the world's longest bike race probably has his or her own answer.

Outstanding physical fitness and mental strength definitely form the basis, plus a well-rehearsed, flexible and professional team takes care of logistics, support, catering and break arrangements.

But an often underestimated factor is the strategy: There is not necessarily much heroic about having to endure more pain than necessary during the race. Outgrowing oneself, the oft-cited fighting spirit, persevering despite sleep deprivation and almost unbearable discomfort are often just the result of inadequate planning. With an approach tailored to one's own abilities, the stresses and strains can be significantly reduced.

Simply copying the strategy from winners or record runs of others and adopting it for yourself without considering your own strengths and weaknesses often leads to failure - or at least to unnecessary suffering.

In fact, during my fastest RAAM participations, I didn't take 20-minute power naps until after 36 and 48 hours each, and took my first real sleep break of one hour after crossing the Rocky Mountains, after two and a half days of riding. This strategy may seem risky, but it was the step-by-step result of the experiences of the previous years - my team and I had approached it in the long term. In addition, we had hardly any unfavorable weather when I set my course record in 2014, an experienced team that had already participated in a total of 42 RAAMs, and an ideal race course that spurred me on psychologically. If a rookie were to do the same, there's a pretty good chance that strategy wouldn't work.

For me, true winners are those who realistically assess their abilities and have the courage to develop tactics that suit them, and then implement them with the necessary flexibility. Kurt's unusual strategy of taking longer breaks in motels at the beginning instead of short stops in the motorhome in order to make up ground at the end with more reserves than the competition was a complete success. To start the RAAM naively, to push yourself beyond your limit and to fight for the finish under great strain and without fun, makes the RAAM even more difficult and harder than it already is.

Because in the end, the positive experiences should outweigh the negative ones at RAAM: the team spirit, the impressive landscapes, the joy of cycling, the fair competition, the achievement of seemingly impossible goals.

Kurt Matzler is an inspiration to me: he has worked his way up to this huge project in small steps over the years, has accepted various setbacks with patience and tenacity and has learned from them. Kurt has already gained valuable experience on the course as a participant in the "Team Rotary RAAMs Polio" four-man relay teams and has built a crew around him, which he has formed into a well-coordinated team with his clear goal, in which everyone trusts and inspires each other to do their best.

The art of putting the team together is to lead the way as a leader, to formulate the goal and to live like this every day in preparation in order to get closer to the goal, and thus also to carry the team along and motivate it. In the race, however, you are then supposed to relinquish control to the crew and focus only on your job - pedalling, eating, drinking and staying awake - and trust the team. Leaving the decisions to the crew is not easy and also a learning process. But this letting go and delegating is essential to being able to finish a race like RAAM. An overtired athlete can't make clear and sensible decisions.

Christoph Strasser: Six-time winner of the Race Across America, record holder of the RAAM and 24h world record holder (Photo: Lex Karelly)

But Kurt's achievements off the bike are also impressive: it's great to see the donations he and his team have handed over for good causes. A strong network, creative ideas and persistence in implementation made it possible to raise a total of more than four million dollars to eradicate polio. I am especially pleased that I was able to contribute with the proceeds of my multimedia lecture at the University of Innsbruck. This day was of course organized by Kurt Matzler himself.

At this point I would also like to thank Kurt: for the friendly connection, for the mutual support, and also for the conversation we had about his RAAM in our "Sitzfleisch" podcast.

I wish all readers a lot of joy with this book and a lot of strength and fun while working on their own goals! Be inspired by the clever strategic approach and enjoy the lively narrative of one of the greatest sporting adventures there is!

Best regards,

Christoph Strasser

Preface

The Race Across America is considered the toughest and longest cycling race in the world and the toughest sports competition ever. When I first heard about it, I couldn't even imagine the massive scale of this race, the athletes seemed "superhuman" to me. It was only over time, as I became more familiar with ultracycling and cycled longer and longer distances, that the Race Across America moved into the realm of possibility. At some point, I made the decision to try. The unimaginable became conceivable, the dimensions graspable, and successful participation realistic. I learned that limits exist only in the mind. What becomes imaginable becomes feasible. In the meantime, I am convinced that every healthy person could take part in the Race Across America. What is needed is the enthusiasm for this great goal, the willingness to train for years, enormous discipline and mental strength. The right team that shares this enthusiasm and is willing to fight together for the goal is indispensable.

Many people before me have written about what the recipe for success is in order to achieve peak performance. Apart from biographies of athletes who have made it to the top in their sport and countless guides to mental strength in life and work, there seems to be a real boom in performance-enhancing gadgets and training methods in the field of sports and fitness science. After years of preparation, I can say that the road is a long one and it takes more than talent to be among the elite. Motivation and inspiration are all well and good, but dreaming big - without a plan or structure - has hardly helped any athlete reach the podium.

In this book I tell the story about the race of my life. I tell of my years of preparation, of my strategy and my plans, of the physical and mental challenges, of the highs and lows.

As a professor of strategic management, I deal professionally with the question of what makes companies particularly successful. In this book, I change my perspective. I try to find answers to the question of what helps us as people, as athletes or managers, to achieve top performance. My experiences from the Race Across America, as well as my reflections on my professional journey, led me to believe that it is mainly the mindset - the high performance mindset. I am convinced that we can learn a lot from extreme sports for our life and for our professional career. In addition to the story about the race of my life, in this book you will find eleven lessons I have learned over time. Eleven lessons that can push us to peak performance and shape our high performance mindset.

This book would never have happened without the support of many people. The Race Across America is a 5000-kilometer individual time trial. The solo rider is in the foreground. But behind the rider is a team, without whose support such a project would never be possible. My team Rotary RAAMs Polio gave everything in the preparation and during the race to support me. Without my wife Ruth Brandstätter, my crew chief Zoltàn Bogdàn and my world class crew with Bill Clark, Martin Ebster, Liane Fendt, Darlene McKenzie, Bob McKenzie, Florian Phleps, Alexandra Podpeskar, Hubert Siller, Balàsz Vargas and

Roland Volderauer the race of my life would never have happened - I am infinitely grateful! Andi Zemann, Irene Rohregger and Julia Kovacs supported me from Austria. Martin Böckle from TV station K19 got up early in the morning every day during the race to edit the video footage and finish the TV reports. Martin Roseneder, as my press spokesman, made sure that our project - which was also a big fundraising project - got the appropriate broad exposure. I would also like to thank my physiotherapist Anna Entleitner, who has kept me fit over the years. Markus Waldhart from F7 Training did a great job as my trainer. I would like to thank all those who supported me in completing the manuscript, especially Ruth, Alex and Liane as well as Andrea Mayr and Bob McKenzie.

I dedicate this book to my two sons Maximilian and Felix, who go their own ways with determination and enthusiasm and whose successes impress me very much and make me proud.

Dear reader - now I hope you enjoy reading this book. I am happy if the race of my life inspires you and you take away one or the other idea. Boundaries exist only in the mind! With the right mindset, you can do almost anything!

Innsbruck, June 2023

The race of my life

Eleven days, five hours and 50 minutes. Eleven days, five hours and 50 minutes to cross the American continent in the toughest and longest bike race in the world: 4880 kilometers, 42,300 meters of climbing, twelve states, four time zones, two deserts, three mountain ranges. 51 degrees Celsius maximum temperature in the Mojave Desert. Rain and freezing temperatures on Wolf Creek Pass, the highest point of the race at 3300 meters. Through a tornado in Colorado, 1000 kilometers of fierce crosswinds in the Great Plains, dangerous truck traffic on the highways. Eleven days of sleep deprivation to the point of hallucinations. Excruciating pain, technical breakdowns again and again. Per day an average of 432 kilometers, 3800 meters of climbing, about 50,000 pedal strokes, about 13,000 calories burned, about 14.5 liters of sweat lost. Between two and three hours of sleep - per day -, for eleven days. After years of preparation, on June 25, 2022, around 11 p.m., my dream came true - I am a solo finisher of the Race Across America (RAAM), and I stand on the podium of the longest and toughest bike race in the world with third place in my age category. After years of preparation and indescribable exertion, I am now one of the world's best long-distance cyclists.

The 40-year history of the Race Across America has produced no more than about 400 finishers of this brutal race. Less than 50 percent of solo starters finish each year. Of the rookies, those trying it for the first time, less than 30 percent make it. There are fewer Race Across America finishers overall than there are conquerors of Mount Everest in any given year.

In 1953, Edmund Hillary and Tenzing Norgay were the first to climb the highest mountain on earth. Since Reinhold Messner and Peter Habeler conquered the mountain without oxygen in 1978, the number of successful ascents of Mount Everest has risen continuously - to a peak of 878 in 2019.[1] There have been more than 300 deaths so far. About 10,000 people have stood on the highest point on Earth - including Austrian Wolfgang Fasching in 2001. But the extreme athlete is better known as an eight-time finisher of the Race Across America and a three-time winner of that race. His comparison of RAAM with Mount Everest: Mount Everest is more dangerous, but the Race Across America is tougher.[2]

Race Across America - the route.[3]

RAAM is the toughest sports competition of all. This was concluded by a commission of experts, commissioned by Outside magazine. The criteria taken into account for these ratings were: a) the length of the competition, b) the degree of difficulty, c) the mental challenge, and d) the ratio of cost to DNF (did not finish). The Race Across America received 676.2 points, with the Vendée Globe Around the World Sailing Race (675 points) behind it, followed by the Iditarod Trail Sled Dog Race (417.5 points). Ironman Hawaii came in at 67.2 points.[4] RAAM is 30 percent longer than the Tour de France, and finishers complete it in about half the time. It is not a stage race, but an individual time trial. Once the starting gun goes off, the clock ticks incessantly - at every short rest, at every sleep break, at every stop at every traffic light. Drafting is forbidden, and the cyclist and his team must take care of themselves along the entire route. This includes food and drink as well as medical care and the necessary equipment. The route is precisely defined. The participants are monitored by GPS transmitters and race officials. A detailed 60-page set of rules leaves no room for interpretation. If you break one of the many rules - for example, if you don't stop at a stop sign - you will receive a time penalty. Five time penalties result in disqualification. The race demands everything from the cyclist and the accompanying team: years of planning and preparation, top physical form, mental strength. Enormous capacity for suffering, stress tolerance and logistical masterstrokes are absolute prerequisites to have any chance at all of finishing. The financial and organizational outlay should also not go unmentioned - you have to reckon with a budget of around 50,000 euros.

My twelve-member support team and I achieved extraordinary results. Not only did we finish third in the master class (sixth overall), our participation raised over 1.2 million euros in donations for polio eradication. Unbelievable - the longer the race goes back, the more aware I become of what we actually achieved.

My cycling career

I have always been sporty. As a teenager, I was a track and field athlete - mainly a high jumper, but also a decathlete. I played soccer on my village team, was on my school's basketball team and volleyball team, and - which wasn't particularly strenuous from an athletic point of view - I was a curler. Seven to eight training sessions a week were normal for me. My performance in school did not shine particularly brightly during this time, which worried me less, but more my mother again and again. Unnecessarily, as it turned out. I graduated from high school as second best in my school. I enjoyed studying business administration at the University of Innsbruck even more. I financed it by myself and worked full-time during the vacations and very often on weekends during the semester as a waiter. 70 to 80 hours a week of work and study were not uncommon. There was never any vacation. I remember one summer when I worked for three months - ten to twelve hours a day, seven days a week - and at the same time prepared for a major economics exam in the fall. I found the time to do it during my two-, three-hour break in the afternoon. I easily got to 100 hours a week that summer. It was exhausting, but worth it. I passed the exam with flying colors.

Working as a waiter taught me one thing: efficiency. I had to take care of the guests in the restaurant, in the bar and on the terrace. Often, I could only manage the work by running the distance from the bar to the terrace! I could only get the job done by doing several things at once - I had gotten into the habit of never running empty-handed, of making every second count. This attitude shaped my entire work life and later my training for the Race Across America. In winter, I regularly reeled off 5000 kilometers on the indoor bike. To make use of this time as well, I acquired a lectern and did my reading while training. I read about 15 to 20 technical books and countless scientific papers a year while training, and I also educated myself via podcasts, videos and audio books.

But back to my student days. The enormous time burden of studies and work left no minute for sports. I was far removed from the former daily workouts and became a downright sports muffin. After graduation, Professor Hans Hinterhuber immediately offered me an PhD position at the Department of Management. Since I was used to working seven days a week, I went straight on like that. Witha, my girlfriend at the time and later the mother of my two sons, was not exactly enthusiastic and tried to convince me that there was something else in life besides work. For me it was normal to work on Saturdays and Sundays. Besides doing research for my dissertation and teaching at the university, I got a lot of opportunities to work on projects, design workshops for companies, give talks, etc. I published my first book two years before I finished my dissertation. It was not uncommon for me - because there was no end to the work - to spend all night preparing a seminar day, take a quick shower in the morning, and then, without having slept a minute, teach a group of executives all day.

Although this rhythm of life didn't bother me, I realized that I was missing something important: sports. Martin, a friend of mine, got me into mountain biking, and a little later, I was 28, he got me a racing bike. It was the Colnago Master Olympic, the training bike of the world champion Maurizio Fondriest. His mechanic had a bike store in Innsbruck. A few friends of mine were training for the Styrkeprøven - the great trial of strength - a race held annually on the solstice in Norway. The route is 540 kilometers long from Trondheim to Oslo - non-stop. About 4000 meters of climbing have to be covered. Since I trained with them again and again, they finally asked me if I would like to do the race together with them. I had no idea about road cycling, only trained a few kilometers and of course didn't trust myself to do this race. Hubert, one of my friends, then jokingly said: "That's quite easy, Trondheim is in the north, Oslo in the south. That means it's always descending anyway!"

With that, I was convinced - after all, it had to be fun with these guys!

The race started on June 18, 1999. Since you can't train well on the road in Tyrol in winter, I didn't start my training until February, March. I had just over 2000 kilometers in my legs until Styrkeprøven. Martin, Hubert, Markus and Peter took the time to drive to Trondheim with the camper. I flew there just before the race. We trained a bit, but actually we enjoyed more the landscape so shortly before the race. And because we were so cool, we drank red wine and smoked cigars in the evenings. And because we were not only cool, but also smart, we knew that we would need a lot of energy, i.e. calories, for the race. The evening before the race, we went out to eat - steak with fries, dessert -, and of course red wine again. At 11 p.m. we were at the hotel. The sun was still shining, and it was bright in the room. We could hardly darken it. Belly full and in the bright room I slept more badly than well. At some point it was 6 o'clock. We got up, went to the start, and off we went. The weather was good at first, but after a few hours it started to rain. On Dovrefjell, the highest point, it was snowing. The race was incredibly long, it became incredibly hard. But somehow we made it to the finish after more than 20 hours. I've never been so exhausted.

For the time being, that was the end of long-distance racing. It wasn't until 2007 that I decided to take part in a race again. My friend Alex brought me to the Ötztaler Radmarathon: for many the accolade in cycling, 235 kilometers and 5500 meters of altitude. I crossed the finish line with a time of just over ten hours. Six more times I took part - the last time in 2014, when I reached my goal of completing the course in less than nine hours. That closed the Ötztaler chapter for me.

I became interested in longer distances again. And as luck would have it, Rotary brought me to my next project in 2013. Meinhard Huber, the president of the Cycling to serve Austria Fellowship, organized a long-distance ride from Weiz in Styria to Bregenz in Vorarlberg - from the 1910 District Conference to the 1920 District Conference (Rotary Austria is divided into two districts). We wanted to cover the more than 600 kilometers and about 8000 meters of climbing in 30 hours while collecting donations for the eradication of polio. It was during this long-distance bike ride that I first came into direct contact with the Race Across America. One of the participants was the

Hungarian RAAM solo finisher Ferenc Szönyi. He had heard about our project and joined us. On the way he told me that he had already cycled from Hungary to Weiz before, was now accompanying us, wanted to cycle around Lake Constance the next day and then back to Hungary - unimaginable for me. We reached Bregenz after about 30 hours. I said to Meinhard at the finish line that I would be there again if he organized something like this again. This statement would later bring me to Team Rotary RAAMs Polio, a four-man team that raced the 2016 RAAM in the relay.

But before that, I went to Norway once again for the Styrkeprøven. I joined the German Vitargo team that wanted to finish the race in 18 hours. A day or two before the start, I met the team members in Trondheim. We had a short team meeting where the race strategy was explained. Every two hours there would be a two-minute break, ten seconds before the end of the break a whistle would sound and someone would count down. If you were not on the bike at zero, the group started without you. If you missed the start whistle, you lost not only the slipstream of the group, but also the support vehicle, which contained food, clothing and spare materials. In those two minutes of rest, everything had to be done - pee break, refill food, refill bottles, change clothes. Extremely stressful, but successful. Not everyone finished, but together with a few teammates I managed the 18 hours at an average of about 30 km/h. Once we arrived in Oslo, we spent some time at the finish line. Then I had to pack and allowed myself three or four hours of sleep in the hotel before leaving for the airport and traveling on to Oxford University, where I gave a talk the next day ...

Sometime in late 2015, I was contacted by Meinhard Huber, the president of the Cycling to Serve Fellowship, which had organized the long-distance bike ride for fundraising purposes in 2013. He told me that Bob McKenzie, a Rotarian from Tulsa, Oklahoma, was in the process of putting together a team for the 2016 Race Across America to compete in a four-man relay. With this project, he wanted to raise funds to eradicate polio. I immediately signalled to Meinhard that I was interested. I was physically in a good shape, and there were still a few months to go before the start. Nico Endres, the president of the worldwide fellowship Cycling to Serve, put me in touch with Bob McKenzie. I contacted Bob, showing great interest and describing my racing experience to date. In the last sentence, I made it clear that - living in the heart of the Alps - I loved mountain trails and long climbs. Bob McKenzie replied that this was a good match because he preferred long descents. We agreed to keep in touch, and a few weeks later, on January 28, 2016, at 3:51 p.m., I received his reply:

> "Hi Kurt, Thanks for being patient with me and my questions. We would like to invite you to join 'Team Rotary RAAMs Polio'! Let me know your decision and we will pick up from there.
>
> In the Best Bonds,
>
> Bob McKenzie"

I was on the team! My first Race Across America project began. I intensified my training, started looking for sponsors, fundraising and got more involved with the race. I began reading books about RAAM, searching for videos on YouTube, preparing myself for the adventure. One YouTube video from a team in 2013 particularly impressed me: it described a team of four losing a rider in the desert. In the heat, he had drunk too much water, suffered "water poisoning" and ended up in the hospital for two days. Afterwards, he immediately had himself taken by car to his team, which had probably cycled far more than 1,500 kilometers in the meantime, and rode along again.

Crazy, I thought to myself. Later it turned out that this Randy Jackson was part of Team Rotary RAAMs Polio 2016.

Race Across America 2016-2019

In the months leading up to the start, we coordinated via Skype meetings. I was the only European on the team; Meinhard Huber was on the support team. The rest of the team consisted of Americans - all friends of Bob. They organized everything on site, my only job was to train and collect donations. Meinhard and I flew to Oceanside in California a few days before the start. We arrived on Wednesday, and the race started on Saturday, June 18. We chose a race strategy typical of teams: we split into two teams of two (Randy and Steve, Bob and I) and scheduled eight-hour intervals. During our eight-hour shift, we planned to take turns every 30 minutes, and the eight-hour break was to be used for regeneration, eating, and sleeping. Of course, everything was to be done in a moving motor home, since during the break the other team covered about 240 kilometers and the team taking a break had to be brought to the next changeover point. This required several escort vehicles and a large motor home.

We all started together, then Steve and Randy took over the first leg. My first shift started in Borrego Springs in the desert, around 6 pm. It was unbearably hot: 45 degrees in the shade. During the night it cooled down to about 30 degrees. After a good start, the first big problems came the next day: record heat in the desert with more than 50 degrees Celsius, and the air conditioning of the camper broke down. Sleeping - without air conditioning and in a moving motorhome - became almost impossible for the crew and the racers. And if you did doze off, you were rudely awakened after a few minutes when the motorhome hit a pothole, had to brake abruptly or manoeuvre back and forth in tight spots. In general, you could already be happy if you found a place in the soft bed. Due to the lack of space, we had to take turns and sometimes sleep on the floor of the motorhome. The bed linen was of course not changed. Whoever got a place to sleep could lie down in the bed that was still warm from the previous person. There was no time for cleaning, shower and toilet were soon in a corresponding condition. The condition of the team was also corresponding, we soon all suffered from enormous sleep deprivation. The strategy of Bob, who decided to sleep in one of the support vehicles for the whole race - seven days - didn't help much. Due to jet lag problems, I personally had already slept very little in the nights before the race.

We were all so exhausted that on the third day we rented a hotel room: a room for two hours for eight people in the only hotel far and wide. Again, we slept in rotation - everyone got a bed for about 30 minutes. Of course, this did not work a miracle. The sleep deprivation got so bad that I started hallucinating. One night in the Rocky Mountains, I saw lots of rabbits on the side of the road. With power naps of about 15 minutes, we somehow managed to survive the race, which otherwise went quite well: not a single drop of rain, not a single bike breakdown.

Towards the end, we kept overtaking solo riders. Because of the time limits of twelve days for solo riders and nine days for teams, the solo riders traditionally always start on a Tuesday and the relays on the following Saturday. Teams, of course, are much faster than solo riders, and so towards the end of the race you're always overtaking solo riders who are struggling with sleep deprivation, total exhaustion, and all sorts of health issues. When I passed the first solo rider in the early hours of the morning two days before we crossed the finish line, he was cycling on the flat at about 15 km/h. He was cycling out of the saddle - he probably couldn't sit anymore - with his head down. I spoke to him, he reacted however only at the second time, greeted and mumbled with hoarse voice something incomprehensible, without turning the head to me. A zombie, I thought to myself. I was already pretty exhausted as a team rider, but a solo participation in this race? That was unimaginable to me. How could anyone do such a thing to themselves?

We reached Annapolis after seven days, one hour and 16 minutes, placing second in our age category (50 to 60). The donation result of around 300,000 dollars was also impressive. At the finish line I met the solo finisher Martin Bergmeister from South Tyrol. He later gave me some valuable tips for my solo ride, and I learned a lot from his experiences at RAAM in 2016.

Barely four weeks after the finish, we made the decision to try again in 2017. Since Randy Jackson did not want to race again due to health problems during the 2016 race, we were looking for a replacement. I immediately thought of Andi Zemann, a Tyrolean friend and also a Rotarian, and asked him if he could imagine doing RAAM with us in the team. He immediately agreed. The game started all over again. We needed about

40,000 euros in sponsorship, had to put together a support team, plan, organize, fundraise and train - about 15,000 kilometers in one year. The year went by quickly. When I was on a 300-kilometer training ride from Bolzano to Bologna in Italy in April 2017, I got bad news. For health reasons, Andi could not come along! Less than two months before the start. Everything was already organized, the hotels were reserved, all flights booked. How could we find a replacement at such short notice? Since my wife Ruth was scheduled to be in the support team, our choice fell on her. Ruth was as enthusiastic a road cyclist as I was. She had raced the Ötztaler Radmarathon several times and had been training with me for years. But I also knew that she didn't want to race anymore. Nevertheless, I asked her. She looked at me with wide eyes and wasn't sure if I was serious. She also wasn't sure if she could do it. My response, "This is like any vacation for us. Six to seven hours on the bike every day for a week. Under somewhat more stringent conditions, that is."

That convinced her. Andi switched to the support vehicle and Ruth to the bike. So we flew to Oceanside a few weeks later. We changed our strategy: No camper van, instead overnight stays in hotels and better change tactics - that should ensure that each of us - team riders and crew - enjoyed about three to four hours of sleep per day. That was significantly better than in 2016. This time, however, the weather conditions were much worse. Again, the temperatures in the desert climbed up to 50 degrees, but we had much more wind and lots of rain towards the end of the race. We even fought our way through the remnants of Hurricane Cindy. Still, we were faster than in 2016 and raised over

$500,000 in donations. Ruth handled the race with aplomb, and it was she who suggested we compete again the following year.

Still at the finish line, we decided to participate again in 2018. Markus Mayr from East Tyrol replaced Steve Schoonover, a few new crew members joined us, we further improved our strategy and were again significantly faster! With six days, 18 hours and four minutes, we not only won our category, but set a new course record. For the just over one million dollars in donations we raised to eradicate polio, we received the Lon Haldeman Award, which is given annually to the team that raises the most money for charity.

That we went to the start again as a team of four in 2019 was thus pre-programmed. Like every year, we flew to Oceanside a few days before the start. This time we were even invited to the official RAAM press conference. We had raised about $900,000 in donations by that point, and Bob said in passing, "If we make over a million again, Kurt will ride solo next time!" I didn't take that too seriously, but agreed more in jest. Then during the press conference - I was on stage, Bob in the audience - the moderator surprisingly asked me a question: "Is it true that you'll ride solo next time if you raise over a million dollars in donations again?"

My answer: "Yes, I might consider trying to ride solo ... "

Bob grinned. He hadn't told me before that we had already cracked the million in Oceanside. So the decision was made: Race Across America solo!

But before that, we all had to get through this race in one piece and arrive healthy in Annapolis. By now, we were able to deal well with the usual problems such as heat, sleep deprivation, wind, cold in the Rocky Mountains, rain and breakdowns. We were much faster than in 2018. Everything went as planned - until Ohio. There we experienced the worst case. The entire team communicated via a WhatsApp group. After a short power nap, I glanced at my smartphone. Someone had posted an audio recording that I couldn't make any sense of at first: a strange noise that lasted for seconds. At the end of the recording, you could hear Andi asking his wife Irene if she was okay.

"Yeah, you too?" Her voice sounded panicked.

After that, a photo. A car, in the middle of the highway, lying on its roof - total loss.

Only at second glance did I realize that it was a car from our team. Our media team. Andi was just behind the wheel when he got tired on the way to the hotel. They were on the highway and wanted to stop at the next opportunity. It didn't come to that. Microsleep overcame him, he touched the guard rails, the car rolled over, skidded along on its roof for a few seconds and finally came to a halt in the middle of the highway. At the time of the accident, Irene happened to be online in our WhatsApp group, accidentally hit the record button, and everything was on WhatsApp! Both were hanging upside down in their seat belts. Quick-witted, Andi told Irene not to loosen the seatbelt under any circumstances - that could easily have resulted in a broken neck. Andi's second concern was the traffic on the highway - hopefully there wasn't a car coming from behind that couldn't brake in time ... But two truck drivers had observed everything and stood slightly across the lane to shield the accident car. They rushed to help Andi and Irene, who in the meantime had freed themselves. The truck drivers were astonished when the two crawled out of the car lying on its roof - wearing safety vests. One of the many RAAM rules stipulates that crew members must always wear high-visibility vests. And after their mission, the two had not taken off their safety vests. They got out of the car unharmed. The shock, however, was deep and made us realize how dangerous the race could be. The two organized a new rental car and drove after us.

Microsleep: Total loss on the highway. (Photo: Andreas Zemann)

After six days, 14 hours and six minutes, we once again won the race in our category with an average speed of 31.2 km/h and improved our course record once again. With over one million in donations, we were now at over three million dollars total. What a success.

2016	2017	2018	2019
Team	**Team**	**Team**	**Team**
Bob McKenzie (USA)	Bob McKenzie (USA)	Bob McKenzie (USA)	Bob McKenzie (USA)
Randy Jackson (USA)	Steve Schoonover (USA)	Ruth Brandstätter (AUT)	Ruth Brandstätter (AUT)
Steve Schoonover (USA)	Ruth Brandstätter (AUT)	Kurt Matzler (AUT)	Kurt Matzler (AUT)
Kurt Matzler (AUT)	Kurt Matzler (AUT)	Markus Mayr (AUT)	Markus Mayr (AUT)
Crew	**Crew**	**Crew**	**Crew**
David Armstrong (USA)	John Adams (USA)	Bill Clark (USA)	Zoltàn Bogdàn (HUN)
Bill Clark (USA)	Meinhard Huber (AUT)	Meinhard Huber (AUT)	Bill Clark (USA)
Todd Duhon (USA)	Susanne Marth (AUT)	Monika Huber (AUT)	Markus Huber (AUT)
Meinhard Huber (AUT)	Darlene McKenzie (USA)	Ryan Jackson (USA)	Meinhard Huber (AUT)
Ryan Jackson (USA)	Ryan Jackson (USA)	Susanne Marth (AUT)	Monika Huber (AUT)
Marvin Lee (USA)	Ryan Schoonover (USA)	Julia Mayr (AUT)	Michael Istenich (AUT)
Jack McGlumphy (USA)	Irene Rohregger (AUT)	Irene Mayr (AUT)	Randy Jackson (USA)
Darlene McKenzie (USA)	Andi Zemann (AUT)	Rainer Lamprecht (D)	Julia Kovacs (AUT)
Erik Ortega (USA)	Stefan Zemann (AUT)	Darlene McKenzie (USA)	Susanne Marth (AUT)
Linda Ortega (USA)	Jack McGlumphy (USA)	Irene Rohregger (AUT)	Irene Mayr (AUT)
Justyn Rains (USA)		Andi Zemann (AUT)	Hannes Meissl (AUT)
John Robertson (USA)		Stefan Zemann (AUT)	Darlene McKenzie (USA)
			Irene Rohregger (AUT)
			Andi Zemann (AUT)

Team Rotary RAAMs Polio 2016-2019.

Back in Austria, I now started my preparations for my solo debut at the Race Across America. I had already thought about doing the race solo in 2018. However, I didn't really want to venture into it until I passed a few other tests first. I developed a master plan, but I didn't discuss it with anyone at the time. My first test was to be the Race Across Italy, which takes place every year in April. Should I succeed in that, I could venture into the Race Around Austria - 2200 kilometers non-stop around Austria. Should that also be successful, only then did I want to venture to the Race Across America. Even when Bob urged me to make the official decision in 2019 during the RAAM press conference, I had this plan in mind. But the 2019 press conference was the final decision for me and the official go-ahead for the project.

Race Across Italy

The Race Across Italy is one of the qualifying races for RAAM. Since 2013, some of the world's best ultracyclists have been competing there to ride around 800 kilometers and 10,000 meters of climbing non-stop across Italy. For me, it was the perfect first test. The start and finish are in Silvi on the Adriatic coast, near Pescara. Taking place very early in the season, it requires good preparation over the winter. The route goes through the Gran Sasso, where it can be very cold in April, especially in bad weather, on to the other side of Italy to the coast south of Rome and then back again. The many meters of climbing over this short distance are a particular challenge. Meinhard and Monika Huber, who already had a lot of Race Across America experience as crew members, agreed to crew for me.

At the Race Across Italy I got a first taste of the challenges that were to await me at the Race Across America. My finishing time was around 40 hours. That wasn't particularly fast, but for me it was mainly about the experience and getting to the finish line at all. I approached the race very defensively. I only had one 15-minute sleep break in the 40 hours. I rode my S-Works Venge - with no aero bars. That taught me my first lesson. At the finish line, I could no longer feel the little fingers and half of the ring fingers on both hands: carpal tunnel syndrome. The nerves were pinched off by the constant pressure on the hands on the handlebars. It took about three months before I could feel my fingers normally again. Lesson learned: Aero bars in an endurance race is an absolute must to relieve the pressure on the hands. But that wasn't all: two days after the race, I had a presentation at the World Congress of Candle Manufacturers in Barcelona. Once there, my shoulder started to hurt. The lecture was pure agony. The excruciating pain was almost unbearable. A consequence of the Race Across Italy. A cortisone injection and numerous physiotherapy sessions were necessary.

My second lesson taught me to rethink my sleep strategy. Even on a relatively "short" route, sleep deficit is to be expected; the last mountain in Italy became a nightmare for me. However, it was not so much the climb as the descent that caused me problems. I was fighting exhaustion after almost 40 hours continuously on the bike. As soon as the body is no longer in motion and the circulation goes down a bit, i.e. when riding downhill, fatigue overtakes you like a surprise. It was only years later that Monika, then on the crew, told me about the hallucinations I obviously had on the descent. Meinhard and Moni observed how I repeatedly turned my bike to the left. They asked me why I was doing that, and I guess I replied, "There are always people just climbing over the guardrails onto the road. I have to swerve."

At about three in the morning on a deserted mountain road, these careless people were fortunately no more than figments of my brain.

After 41 hours and 15 minutes I was at the finish - 9.5 hours after the first-placed Jean Vanek. Nevertheless, the successful finishing of the Race Across Italy - despite the difficulties - gave me courage for the Race Around Austria.

Race Around Austria 2020

In 2019, I came to about 20,000 training kilometers. That was a formidable increase over the roughly 15,000 kilometers I had trained annually up to that point. I wanted to maintain this training workload for the Race Around Austria (RAA). Since RAAM 2020 was cancelled due to COVID and we therefore did not participate as a relay team, I was able to focus entirely on the RAA. With its 2200 kilometers and over 30,000 meters of climbing around Austria, the Race Around Austria is the longest individual time trial race in Europe and probably the toughest qualifying race for the Race Across America. Except for the record-breaking temperatures in the desert and the long straights in Kansas and Missouri, you can experience pretty much all the challenges you would face at RAAM. A similar set of rules apply, and the demands on the cyclist and crew are enormous. A sleeping and nutrition strategy was needed, and especially in the mountains in the west you have to expect everything - up to snowfall. The statistics for successful Race Around Austria finishers are promising. Those who manage the RAA have an almost 100 percent chance of also being successful at the RAAM.

I started with the planning and preparations about a year before the start. For the crew I could again rely on a proven team: my wife Ruth, Monika and Meinhard Huber, Andi Zemann and Irene Rohregger, Julia Kovacz and Zoltàn Bogdàn, and in East Tyrol Michael Istenich, Heinz Istenich and Hannes Meissl joined them - all with Race Across America experience. I decided on an unusual strategy: no camper van, instead sleep brakes in a hotel and about one and a half hours sleep break per day. This required a lot of planning, but should allow me a better regeneration. So I wanted to do the 2200 kilometers and 30,000 meters of climbing in five days. I had to test this strategy because I also wanted to do the Race Across America this way. Up to the highest mountain, the Großglockner, everything went according to plan. After about 1300 kilometers and almost three days it was time: From Lienz in East Tyrol it was more than 50 kilometers and over 2100 meters of climbing with some very steep passages. In the late afternoon I reached the Fuschertörl, rested for a few minutes and started again immediately. There was a thunderstorm approaching and I wanted to ride the long descent as far as possible in safety and in the dry.

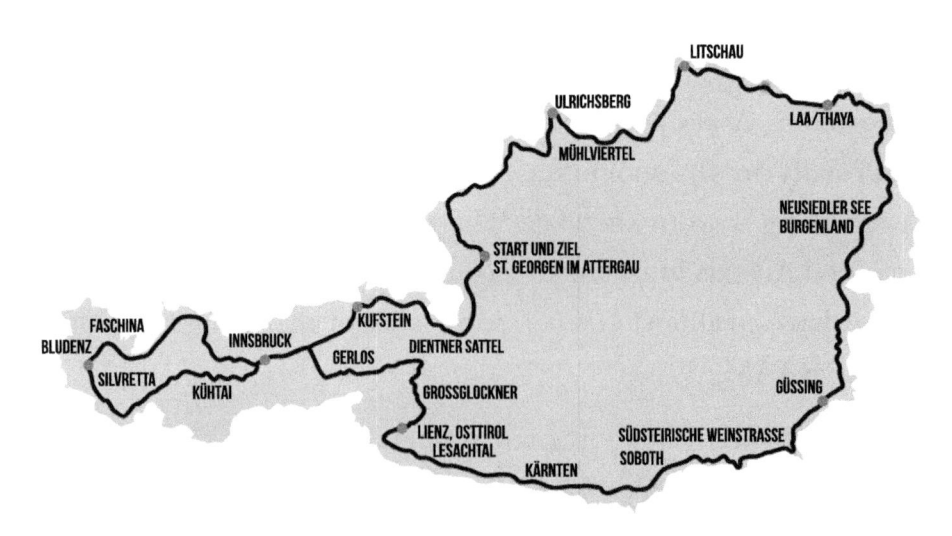

Race Around Austria - the route.[5]

Already almost in the valley, I suddenly ran into a wall of rain. I found a building with a tin canopy and decided to take a short power nap. I wanted to wait until the worst of the thunderstorm had passed. On a mat and well cared for by my crew, I slept warmly covered on the floor for about half an hour. When I woke up, it was only drizzling. Good conditions to get going again. I got on the bike - but suddenly had horrible knee pain that made it almost impossible to continue. I tried, but gave up after a few hundred meters. My crew got me to try again. It was hopeless: the pain was just too much. Julia and Zoli (Zoltàn) suggested a short sleep break in a hotel. I slept there for about two hours, was massaged and given anti-inflammatory tablets. In pain, I got on the bike again. It was raining and I rode through the night to the Gerlos Pass, then through the Ziller Valley towards Innsbruck, where my next sleep break was planned - *only* 100 kilometers. Mentally and physically at the limit, I kept stopping and wanting to give up. Sleep deprivation and pain plagued me. In the Inn Valley I was barely doing 20 km/h on the flat, it was 3 a.m. and I couldn't go on. Zoli and Julia called Andi and Irene. They should come to motivate me, it needed every support now. When I stopped one last time and wanted to give up, Zoli said, "Only 30 kilometers to Innsbruck for the next sleep break, you have to make it!"

I doubted: "Maybe I'll manage that. But after that comes the Kühtai, the Biehlerhöhe and the mountains in Vorarlberg. I'll never make it with this pain!"

Zoli found the right answer: "Forget everything that comes later. Now there is one goal, and that is Innsbruck. There you have a two-hour sleep break. After that, we'll see."

At the hotel in Innsbruck, I woke up by myself after two hours of sleep. I felt good again, and we managed the Kühtai and the rest of the mountains with aplomb. An important lesson: Never think about how far it still is. Always define small intermediate goals!

After five days, two hours and 27 minutes I was at the finish. I was a finisher of the Race Around Austria, and - what was crucial - I had learned a lot in ultracycling again. The sleep and nutrition strategy with liquid food worked, we were able to deal with the knee pain that almost everyone experiences at some point, and the crew supported me at a world-class level. RAAM could come.

The shattered dream

After a one-week regeneration break, I started training again and intensified it. The goal was now about 25,000 training kilometers for this year, including about 5000 on the indoor bike in the winter. In addition, I did my weekly EMS training with Julia and Zoli. Electro muscular stimulation training involves wearing a suit equipped with electrodes that contract the muscle through electrical impulses. It's particularly time-efficient (20 minutes once a week), easy on the joints, and effective because many muscles are trained at the same time. Through EMS training, I was able to strengthen especially the muscle parts of the torso and neck, which are important for cycling but are often neglected. In winter, I also did a lot of long ski tours, which mainly helped me to improve my basic endurance. A structured training plan by Markus Waldhart (F7 Training) required 15 to 25 hours per week.

I started looking for sponsors and a crew again and began booking flights, renting cars and hotels, planning the route, etc. as early as September. Everything went according to plan, I made very good progress in training, and after the first crew meetings it was clear to me that everything was on track. Only one thing worried me: the then US President Donald Trump had issued an entry ban due to COVID-19. Although the COVID situation improved in the spring, there was no lifting of this ban in sight. Therefore, we sought a National Interest Exception, which is granted to individuals whose entry into the U.S. is of national interest. We received confirmation from the

Austrian Ministry of Arts, Culture, Public Service and Sports that we were competitive athletes and that our participation in RAAM was of Austrian national interest. We received support from the Federal Chancellery, two ministries, were in contact with the Austrian Embassy in Washington, with the U.S. Embassy in Vienna and a number of other institutions. Based on the feedback, we had good reason to remain optimistic about our endeavor. However, one week before departure, the entry permit was still not there. Nevertheless, we were already starting to pack. Bob McKenzie and his wife Darlene, who live near Washington D.C., were already setting off in their packed minivan on their 5,000-kilometer drive to Oceanside, where they planned to wait for us. I was just doing a training lap later in the afternoon when I got the news that our National Interest Exception application had been denied. No entry into the USA! No Race Across America 2021, we had to cancel everything a few days before departure. Bob and Darlene, who had been headed for Oceanside for almost a full day headed back home.

Back from my training ride, I sat down on the terrace, opened a bottle of Primitivo 365 (an Italian red wine), took a picture of it, and posted the picture to our RAAM WhatsApp group. Underneath, I wrote, "We're flying in 365 days. Who's in?"

Without exception, all crew members said yes. RAAM was postponed for one year. We could cancel all flights, all rental cars, all 120 hotel rooms for free! The budget for 2022 was saved - at least good news.

Race Around Austria 2021

After this big disappointment I decided to participate once again in the Race Around Austria. Part of my Race Across America crew was there in support (Ruth, Zoli, Julia, my team doctor Alex, Armin, Andi and Irene). They were joined by Raphaela and Matthias from Bellabambi, one of my sponsors, and Michael, Heinz and Hannes from East Tyrol. We wanted to test everything again and be significantly faster than in 2019. I chose the same strategy again (one-and-a-half-hour sleep break per day in a hotel).

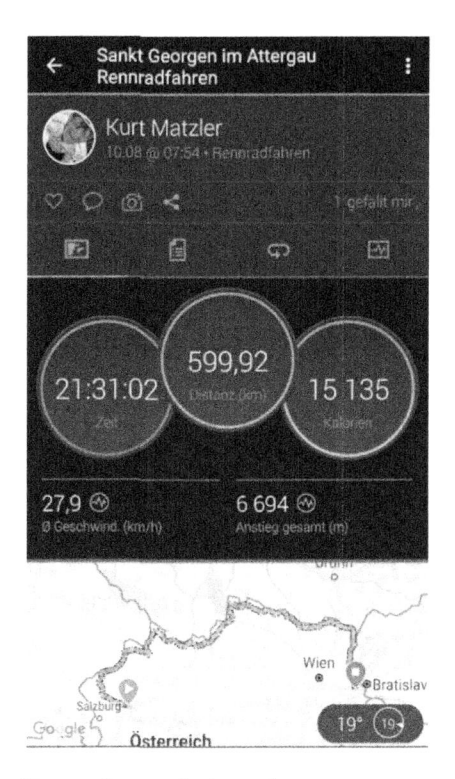

First stage of the Race Around Austria.

I planned the first stage to Deutschaltenburg - 600 kilometers and 7000 meters of climbing.

After 21.5 hours, I reached the hotel at about 8 o'clock in the morning. Still full of adrenaline, however, I couldn't sleep at all, tossing and turning in bed for an hour and a half. I then had my first real sleep break only in Arnoldstein, after 1100 kilometers. Annoying, but again an important lesson for the RAAM. I had to come up with something so that I could actually use every planned sleep break. If that had happened to me at RAAM in the desert, it would have been a disaster.

Just like at the first Race Around Austria, my knees started to ache after the Großglockner in 2021. Unlike the previous year, however, we had learned from our experiences and I was able to deal with the pain much better. Of course, it has to be said in advance that pain is very individual and can have various causes. In ultracycling, it is usually a classic overload reaction of the body. While the musculature and the cardiovascular system can be very well prepared for extensive continuous loads, the knee joint, apart from the bony component, consists mainly of cartilage and tendons - all with very low metabolic activity. All around, the innervating nerves are embedded in the connective tissue. The high continuous mechanical stress and the micro-injuries that accompany it simply exceed the regeneration potential of the structures, the connective tissue hardens, and the conduction of impulses to the nerves is impaired - they cause severe pain. So, in order to boost the exchange of nutrients in the connective tissue, we performed fascia massages from the beginning of the race during every break, no matter how short.

In addition, knowing that the pain was "harmless" made it much easier for me to deal with it.

On the fourth day, another well-known problem appeared: My digestive system caused problems - this revealed a clear disadvantage of my hotel strategy. Without a motorhome, we had to rely on public toilets. What wasn't a major problem in Austria - since there are plenty of gas stations, restaurants, etc. - could become a problem in the U.S. in the desert, in the Rocky Mountains or in Kansas, when you're 200 or 300 kilometers away from any civilization. So I had to come up with something else, since the 60-page RAAM rulebook specifies the following under time penalty: "Public nudity, urination, defecation, lewd or indecent behavior is prohibited."

Everything else was well under control and I finished the race almost half a day faster than last year: four days, 14 hours and 35 minutes, 19.61 km/h average. Now I was really ready for the Race Across America!

The preparations

The crew was ready: three follow vehicles with three people each and a media car with also three crew members. I had already booked flights and rental cars early enough to get the best rates, and Darlene again reserved all 120 hotel rooms. I read every book about RAAM I could find, watched every video, and listened to every podcast. In the meantime, Christoph Strasser, the superstar ultracyclist, and Florian Kraschitzer had launched their podcast, "Sitzfleisch." Every week a new episode appeared, which I mostly listened to while training on the indoor bike: an incredible treasure trove of experiences from "long-distance cyclists" and tips for the RAAM. I now dealt with nutrition, mental training and regeneration much more intensively.

We carried over the strategy and detailed planning from last year. Unlike most riders, I planned for long sleep breaks. My goal was not to win. My goal was to finish the race safely (our fundraising project was one of the main goals), have fun with my crew, and - as much as possible - enjoy this adventure. Since time runs continuously during the race, most RAAM participants consider sleep as lost time, some even as a weakness. Christoph Strasser, the six-time winner and record holder at seven days, 15 hours and 56 minutes, keeps his sleep breaks to an absolute minimum: six to eight hours total! Most people take their first sleep break after 36 hours at the earliest: "After a few days, the body is at the end either way. That's why it doesn't make much sense to sleep a lot at the beginning, and you'd better get as far as you can by the first sleep break," said a RAAM finisher I met with again shortly before departure. If the lack of sleep becomes too great and the risk of microsleep too dangerous, you help yourself with short power naps.

For me, however, this strategy was out of the question. You might get to the finish line faster, but it couldn't be fun that way, and the risk of an accident and total exhaustion wasn't worth it to me. Inspired by two RAAM participants who had done it differently - Michael Nehls[6] and Martin Gruebele[7] - I developed a different strategy. I stuck to their basic ideas and adapted the plan to my goals:

- Four to five hours of rest per day (five-minute rest every three hours, 15-minute rest every nine hours)
- two to three hours of sleep per day
- Sleep breaks for me and my crew in the hotel - no motorhome
- Sleep break over midday, when it is hottest
- first sleep break already after 24 hours
- Nutrition almost exclusively through high-calorie liquid food

I knew that with this strategy I would fall far behind in the first half of the race, but assumed that I would be able to regenerate much better and make up a lot in the second part of the race.

The hotel sleep breaks required detailed planning. Especially in the western U.S. - in the desert, in the Rocky Mountains, in Kansas - the towns are often far more than 100 kilometers apart, and in some of them there is no hotel at all. I spent countless hours planning: How many kilometers could I do in 20 hours? At 50 degrees in the desert, in all kinds of weather, in the mountains? Once I had found the right stage length, I had to find out whether there was a hotel along the route. If there was none far and wide, everything had to be planned anew - shorten or lengthen the route of the previous day, adapt the route of the next day to it, and so on. Finally, my stage plan was fixed: eleven stages between 380 and 551 kilometers in length.

Stage	Start - Finish	Kilometer	Climbing (meters)	km/h average
1	Oceanside (CA) - Salome (AZ)	551	3.420	22,5
2	Salome (AZ) - Flagstaff (AZ)	419	5.280	22,05
3	Flagstaff (AZ) - Cortez (CO)	452	3.180	24,80
4	Cortez (CO) - La Veta (CO)	404	4.230	22,44
5	La Veta (CO) - Montezuma (KS)	529	1.960	24,05
6	Montezuma (KS) - Fort Scott (KS)	506	1.160	26,6
7	Fort Scott (KS) - Washington (MO)	400	2.660	22,9
8	Washington (MO) - Bloomington (IN)	450	1.930	20,05
9	Bloomington (IN) - Athens (OH)	450	2.650	23,08
10	Athens (OH) - Cumberland (MD)	380	4.990	22,35
11	Cumberland (MD) - Annapolis (MD)	395	3.940	26,4

Race Across America Stage Schedule.

I developed a detailed schedule that included target times for each of the more than 50 time stations, and I laid out a plan for the three support vehicles. This included shifts of eight to nine hours for each team.

	DATE	HOTEL	ADDRESS	PHONE NUMBER	RATE	CONF. #	EST. ARR. TIME	DATE OF RESERV.
Car 2	Tue 6/14	Days Inn /Brawley, CA	590 W Main	760-550-9982	1x inc 70.20	657819237	Tue 15:30	11/17/21
Media		Ida			1x inc 70.20	909812582		11/17/21
Car 3	Tue 6/14	Days Inn /Brawley, CA	590 W Main	760-550-9982	1x inc 70.20	367028451	Tue 15:30	11/17/21
Car 1	Tue 6/14	Best Western /Parker, AZ	1012 S Geronimo Ave	928-669-6060	$116.10	159687	Wed 1:00	11/17/21
		Mandy	Late checkout is 12:30		$116,10	159688	Tue/Wed	11/17/21
Car 2	Wed 6/15	Sheflers Inn /Salome, AZ	Hwy 60	928-859-3001	Pd 5/17/22	283433619	Wed 8:30	11/17/21
Media		Jeff (wife is Marjorie)			Visa	0M		11/17/21
Car 3	Wed 6/15	Sheflers Inn /Salome, AZ	Hwy 60	928-859-3001	$180.00	0M	Wed 12:30	11/17/21
Car 1	Wed 6/15	St Michaels /Prescott, AZ	205 W Gurley	928-776-1999	79 + tx	286210	Thurs 2:00	11/23/21
		Skyler - 48 hr can. notice	1 Q in each room		79 + tx	286211	Wed/Thur	11/23/21
		Call ahead to confirm late check out / d.o at noon, but we can request later						
Car 2	Thur 6/16	Best Western	3030 E Rte 66	928-526-2388	116.99 + tax	90023	Thurs 11:00	11/29/21
Media		Pony soldier Inn/Flagstaff	Call the day before to confirm early check-in			90024		11/29/21
Car 3	Thur 6/16	Best Western	3030 E Rte 66	928-526-2388	116.99 + tax	90025	Thurs 12:30	11/29/21
		H / Marji Talia		928-440-5582	REQUESTED EARLY CK IN			
Car 1	Thur 6/16	Hampton / Kayenta, AZ	US Hwy 160	928-697-3170	183.26 + tx	83253918 / 2 rms.	Fri 2:50	11/17/21
		Sierra / Late checkout requested / noon is the lastest they can do			183.26 + tx		Thur/Fri	11/17/21
Car 2	Fri 6/17	Super 8 /Cortez, CO	505 E Main St	970-235-2553	$105.30	100q50960	Fri 11:00	11/29/21
Media		Trisky / Call a day ahead to confirm early check in				084171481		11/29/21
Car 3	Fri 6/17	Super 8 /Cortez, CO	505 E Main St	970-253-2553	$105.30	147826311	Fri 12:30	11/29/21
Car 1	Fri 6/17	West End Lodge/Pagosa Springs	315 Navajo Trail Dr	970-731-2701	$138,17	32215935	Sat 1:45	11/29/21
		booked online	Pd extra for late checkout 1 pm		$276,34	32215844	Fri/Sat	11/29/21
Car 2	Sat 6/18	La Veta Inn, La Veta, CO	103 W Ryus Ave	719-742-5566	149+10+tx ??	4547	Sat 10:15	
Media		she will try to get $149 rate	Hannah	719-989-8959		holds 3 rooms		12/3/21
Car 3	Sat 6/18	La Veta Inn, La Veta, CO	103 W Ryus Ave	719-742-5566	149+10+tx ??		Sat 12:30	
Car 1	Sat 6/18	Corporate East Ulysiys, KS	1110 E Oklahoma Ave	620-356-5010	86 + tx	210870	Sun 4:00	11/30/21
BOOKED SUN 6/19		Lana / CALL AHEAD	In @ 4 am / out at 1 PM they will charge for 1 day.			210871	SUN 6/19	11/30/21

Excerpt from the hotel plan.

The next step was for Darlene to start booking the hotels - an enormous effort with 120 rooms. But not only did the appropriate accommodations have to be found, Darlene called each hotel personally to clarify check-in times. For example, the crew's night shift ended at 9:30 in the morning, so they had to make sure everyone could check in early or stay late.

In addition, I created a detailed course map with estimated arrival times for each Time Station, an elevation profile for each stage with all the specifics on the course, and determined which bike I wanted to ride which section of the course with (time trial bike on the flats, my Tarmac SL7 Speed of Light Collection for the mountains, my S-Works Venge with aero bars as an all-around bike).

I continued my training over the winter at the same intensity, and I prepared myself mentally for RAAM. The long training sessions on the indoor bike - up to five hours, or the high-intensity units during ski touring (e.g. two hours with a 170 heartrate) were particularly hard. Monday was always my rest day - regeneration is an important part of training. During the week, I had units between one and three hours, which I could easily fit in alongside my job, as I spread the three hours between morning and evening. On the weekend, volume was on the agenda. A typical Saturday or Sunday started with two hours on the indoor bike, then I was off on the touring skis twice to the Patscherkofel, Innsbruck's local mountain (about 1250 vertical meters each time), or twice directly from my front door to the Seegrube (about 1050 vertical meters each time). When the roads were dry, I also trained outside on the road bike from time to time - in sub-zero temperatures. So I could test material and clothing for the cold in the Rocky Mountains. On average, I burned more than 4000 calories a day, which I often could hardly eat.

TS	Day	TZ	TS NAME	Miles Raced	Miles To Finish	Miles to next Rest	Miles to next TS	Total hours raced	Race Time Kurt	Hours per shift	Local Time	Car 1 (Bob)	Car 2 (Zoll)	Car 3 (Ruth)
0	Tuesday, 06/14	PDT	Oceanside, CA	0,00	3069,80	342,46	88,40	0,00	16:00		13:00			
1	Tuesday, 06/14	PDT	Borrego Springs, CA	88,40	2981,40	254,06	57,00	5,17	21:10	05:10	18:10	12:30 -		
2	Tuesday, 06/14	PDT	Brawley, AZ	145,40	2924,40	197,06	89,60	10,15	01:50	09:50	22:50	22:30 (10h)	22:00 -	
3	Wednesday, 06/15	MDT	Blythe, AZ	235,00	2834,80	107,46	51,30	16,64	08:00	17:00	06:00		5:30 (7.5h)	
4	Wednesday, 06/15	MDT	Parker, AZ	286,30	2783,50	56,16	56,16	20,27	11:30	20:30	09:30			4:30 -
5	Wednesday, 06/15	MDT	Salome, AZ	342,46	2727,34	0,00	0,00	29,82	15:30	00:30	13:30	Must start at 17:30		14:30 (10h)
Rest	Wednesday, 06/15	MDT	Salome, AZ	342,46	2727,34									
6	Wednesday, 06/15	MDT	Congress, AZ	395,05	2674,75	260,41	52,59		20:30		18:30	16:30 -		
7	Thursday, 06/16	MDT	Prescott, AZ	445,54	2624,26	207,82	50,49	33,91	00:30	04:00	22:30	01:30 (9h)	00:30:00 -	
8	Thursday, 06/16	MDT	Camp Verde, AZ	500,01	2569,79	157,33	54,47	38,03	04:15	07:45	02:15		9:30 (9h)	
9	Thursday, 06/16	MDT	Flagstaff, AZ	602,87	2466,93	102,86	102,86	41,26	07:00	11:30	06:00			8:30 -
Rest	Thursday, 06/16	MDT	Flagstaff, AZ	602,87	2466,93	0,00	0,00	55,17	15:30	19:00	13:30	Must start at 17:30		17:30 (9h)
Start	Thursday, 06/16	MDT	Flagstaff, AZ	602,87	2466,93									
10	Thursday, 06/16	MDT	Tuba City, AZ	677,88	2391,92	281,36	75,01		20:30		18:30	16:30 -		
11	Friday, 06/17	MDT	Kayenta, AZ	749,71	2320,09	206,35	71,83	69,63	00:45	04:15	22:45	01:30 (9h)	0:30 - 9:30	
12	Friday, 06/17	MDT	Mexican Hat, UT	794,42	2275,38	134,52	44,71	65,08	05:45	09:15	03:45		(9h)	
13	Friday, 06/17	MDT	Montezuma Creek, UT	834,01	2235,79	89,81	39,59	67,83	08:20	11:50	06:20			8:30 -
14	Friday, 06/17	MDT	Cortez, CO	884,23	2185,57	50,22	50,22	70,69	10:50	14:20	08:50			17:30 (9h)
Rest	Friday, 06/17	MDT	Cortez, CO	884,23	2185,57	0,00	0,00	79,77	14:45	18:15	12:45	Must start at 17:45		
Start	Friday, 06/17	MDT	Cortez, CO	884,23	2185,57									
15	Saturday, 06/18	MDT	Durango, CO	928,41	2141,39	251,36	44,18		19:45		17:45	16:30 -		
	Saturday, 06/18	MDT	DURANGO, CO CUT-OFF = 81 hours	928,41	2141,39	207,18	0,00	82,94	23:00	03:15	21:00	01:30 (9h)		
	Saturday, 06/18	MDT					54,31	81 hours						
16	Saturday, 06/18	MDT	Pagosa Springs, CO	982,72	2087,08	152,87	47,97	87,11	03:00	07:15	01:00		0:30 - 9:30	
17	Saturday, 06/18	MDT	South Fork, CO	1030,69	2039,11	104,90	46,59	90,67	05:40	09:55	03:40		(9h)	
18	Saturday, 06/18	MDT	Alamosa, CO	1077,28	1992,52	58,31	58,31	93,76	09:45	14:00	07:45			8:30 -
19	Saturday, 06/18	MDT	La Veta, CO	1135,59	1934,21	0,00	0,00	102,80	13:50	18:05	11:50			17:30 (9h)
Rest	Saturday, 06/18	MDT	La Veta, CO	1135,59	1934,21									
Start	Saturday, 06/18	MDT	La Veta, CO	1135,59	1934,21									
20	Saturday, 06/18	MDT	Trinidad, CO	1201,00	1868,80	328,69	65,41		18:50		16:50	16:30 -		
21	Sunday, 06/19	MDT	Kim, CO	1272,31	1797,49	263,28	71,31	106,90	23:50	05:00	21:50	01:30 (9h)		
22	Sunday, 06/19	MDT	Walsh, CO	1340,66	1729,14	191,97	68,35	111,70	03:45	08:55	01:45		0:30 - 9:30	
23	Sunday, 06/19	SDT	Ulysses, KS	1394,82	1674,98	123,62	54,16	115,90	08:00	13:10	06:00		(9h)	
24	Sunday, 06/19	SDT	Montezuma, KS	1444,98	1624,82	69,46	50,16	119,40	11:20	17:30	10:20			8:30 -
Rest	Sunday, 06/19	SDT	10598 Ford Ensign Rd, Dodge City	1464,82	1605,52	19,30	19,30	124,40	14:50	21:00	13:50			17:30 (9h)
	Sunday, 06/19					0,00	0,00		15:50	22:00	14:50			

Excerpt from the schedule.

53

I was looking forward to spring and the first long training sessions outside. Starting in March, I was finally able to do my intervals on the road - in the evenings when it was dark, I rode countless times from Innsbruck over the Höhenstraße to the Hungerburg (about 300 meters of climbing). The road is illuminated and therefore ideal for intervals, even at night. The training volume increased and it became harder and harder. It wasn't unusual for me to have lectures all day - until 5:30 pm. After that, I had to get on the bike for another three hours. In April and May it often rained, then I got on the bike straight from the lecture hall and sometimes rode for three hours in the rain and came home completely soaked in the dark. I looked at it as mental training and kept telling myself, "If this is too much for you, don't even bother flying to Oceanside!"

Training with lead weights on the helmet to strengthen the neck muscles. (Photo: Kurt Matzler)

Orthopedic problems	Shermer's Neck (failure of the neck muscles) Saddle sores (abscesses, open skin, pain) Knee joint overload Swelling of the feet Overloading of the wrists (pain, numbness) Back problems
Heat	Dehydration, comatose states Sunstroke Water poisoning
Gastrointestinal problems	Stomach upset, gastritis, heartburn, dehydration Diarrhea to dehydration and electrolyte disturbances to comatose states
Fatigue	Demotivation due to excessive lack of sleep Accidents due to microsleep Paranoid states due to overwork and sleep deprivation
Speed too low	Decrease in performance due to fatigue Insufficient preparation Lack of athleticism and/or motivation
Problems in the crew	Quarrel/problem due to confinement and lack of sleep Accident Escort vehicle hits cyclist
Time penalties	Disqualification after the fifth time penalty
Respiratory tract	Drying of the mucous membranes up to pulmonary hemorrhage Respiratory tract infection (transition from dry desert to cold, humid Rocky Mountains)
Motivation problems	Exhaustion, disagreements in the team, pain, lack of mental strength, navigational errors

DNF Causes.[8]

In addition to the training, the planning and the organization, I dealt intensively with all the difficulties that could arise during the race and lead to failure. The podcast "Sitzfleisch" by

Christoph Strasser and Florian Kraschitzer, which I mentioned earlier, and the video documentaries of RAAM finishers Christoph Strasser, Martin Bergmeister, Markus Brandl, Gerhard Gulewicz, Michael Nehls, Xandi Meixner, Matt Hoffmann and Max Sala were particularly helpful. I read the race diaries of Christoph Strasser,[9] Guido Löhr,[10] David Misch,[11] Martin Gruebele,[12] Alex Gepp,[13] Srinivas Gokulnath,[14] Karl Traunmüller,[15] Marshall Reeves,[16] Jim Rees[17] and the mental guides of Thomas Jaklitsch[18] and Wolfgang Fasching.[19] I worked through technical literature on long-distance cycling, especially the books by Hughes and Kehlenbach[20] and by Jobson and Irvine.[21]

A good source was the book by Michael Nehls,[22] who systematically elicited all the reasons that could lead to failure at RAAM. For each of the DNF (Did not Finish) reasons, I looked for solutions and countermeasures in the videos and race diaries.

The result was the appropriate physical and mental training and a series of checklists for my support during the race.

The winter months passed quickly, everything seemed to be on track. In spring, however, the first problems arose. Julia, my EMS trainer and physiotherapist, who had already been at RAAM and Race Around Austria, had to cancel her participation in the support team. She had started a physiotherapy study and had big exams during the week of RAAM. Zoli found a replacement, his friend Balàsz from Hungary stepped in. An avid road cyclist himself and a good mechanic, he fit in well with the team. Then we also had to do without Armin, who had accompanied me at the Race Around Austria. Only about two weeks before the start we found a replacement. Liane, a good friend of ours, agreed to join us, but could not fly to the USA until the day of the start because she was at a Rolling Stones concert in Amsterdam. At the last minute the team was complete. We were ready to go.

RACE ACROSS AMERICA 2022 - TEAM ROTARY RAAMS POLIO

RACER
Kurt Matzler

CREW
Zoltàn Bogdàn (Hungary - Crew Chief)
Ruth Brandstätter (Austria)
Bill Clark (USA)
Martin Ebster (Austria)
Liane Fendt (Austria)
Darlene McKenzie (USA)
Bob McKenzie (USA)
Florian Phleps (Austria)
Alexandra Podpeskar (Austria)
Hubert Siller (Austria)
Balàsz Vargas (Hungary)
Roland Volderauer (Austria)

Physically, I felt in top shape. The training had been very effective. One of my favorite routes was the Karwendelrunde (about 180 kilometers). I rode it regularly with several 30-minute intervals at 300 watts - in the basic endurance heart rate. The "Höll", you may know it from the 2018 World Cycling

Championships in Tyrol, with a maximum gradient of 28 percent was usually the end of my training rides on the way home, I also rode this climb in the basic endurance heart rate. The performance test on May 28, 2022, finally confirmed top form: my FTP was just under 380 watts (FTP=Functional Threshold Power, i.e., the maximum wattage you can keep constant for an hour), and my maximum oxygen uptake (VO2 max) was 65.

Leadership Lesson 1: Discipline - It's easier to hold your principles 100 percent of the time than it is to hold them 98 percent of the time!

"Strength does not come from physical capacity. It comes from an indomitable will," Mahatma Gandhi said. If there's one thing you can learn from extreme athletes, it's discipline. Participating in the world's longest and toughest cycling race, the Race Across America, requires years of preparation. The training is at least as hard as the race itself. My training workload for RAAM was enormous: over 100,000 kilometers in five years, over one million meters of climbing, between 15 and 30 hours of training per week. If you have to balance that with a full-time job, you need willpower and stamina. Focusing for years on just one big goal and subordinating everything else to it requires iron discipline - my life consisted of work, training and sleep. In my everyday life as well as in my job and in my free time, preparing for RAAM was my top priority; if I couldn't answer yes to the question "Will this bring me closer to my goal?", I gave it up. My daily routine, my weekends, and my vacations were focused on this one, big goal, a goal that was far away for a long time. During the first few years of preparation, I kept having doubts as to whether I could make it at all. Only gradually did the certainty grow that I had physically and mentally acquired the prerequisites for a successful finish.

A guiding principle of Clayton Christensen, professor at Harvard University, shaped my attitude towards training: "It's easier to hold your principles 100 percent of the time than it is to hold them 98 percent of the time!"[23] Every two weeks, I received detailed training specifications from Markus Waldhart of F7 Training. I tried to fulfill the training plans 100 percent, I did not allow the slightest deviation. On the contrary, I usually trained a little more than required at the beginning of the week in case something came up during the week. Since that was almost never the case, I was almost always above target with my training.

If my training plan called for a seven-hour ride and I came back after my training round after only six hours and 45 minutes, I put in an extra round or rode up and down the street in front of my house until the seven hours were full. If my plan called for three hours of sober training on the indoor bike, I got up early and trained on the indoor bike at home. Not two hours and 58 minutes, not two hours and 59 minutes, but exactly three hours: "It's easier to stick to a principle 100% than 98%!" The first small deviation from the training plan, the first exception, is difficult; the second already a little easier. And the more often you violate a principle, the harder it is to keep it in the future.

Morale erodes very slowly at the beginning, but then suddenly very quickly.

Discipline is also an important virtue during the race. For example, the 60-page rulebook stipulates that the cyclist and his support vehicle must stop at every stop sign. Anyone who violates the rule - and this is checked by race officials - is given a time penalty. Some stop signs are located "in the middle of nowhere," at deserted intersections in the desert, on lonely mountain roads, or somewhere in the vastness of Kansas. Especially at night, when there is not a car to be seen for miles, when there is absolutely no danger and no Race Official in sight, the temptation is great not to stop and simply take the momentum across the intersection. But again, "It's easier to hold your principles 100 percent of the time than it is to hold them 98 percent of the time" Breaking a rule the first time does take some getting over. The second time is a little easier, and soon it becomes a habit. I participated in the Race Across America five times, four times as part of a team and once as a solo rider. Not once was there a time penalty against us. It was always important for us to follow all the rules with extreme discipline. There are not many teams that have participated in RAAM multiple times and come through without a time penalty, maybe we are the only one.

Discipline is not just a Puritan virtue; it is a key trait and foundation for success in virtually all areas of life.[24] Scientific research on self-control and discipline began in the 1960s with psychologist Walter Mischel's well-known experiments on impulse control and delay of gratification in young children. In his famous marshmallow experiments, young children were asked into a room. They were given a marshmallow and the researchers told the children that they would leave the room for a certain amount of time. Then, if they returned after about 15 minutes and the child had not eaten his marshmallow, he would get a second one. If the child could not resist the temptation and had eaten the marshmallow, then there would be no second one. The researchers observed the children's reactions. Some distracted themselves by singing a song, others made up a game, still others covered their eyes or simply tried not to look. It was a tough test for young children: about a third ate the marshmallow immediately, a third managed to resist temptation for a few minutes, and about a third held out until the end.[25] Years later, when Walter Mischel examined what had become of the children who had self-control at the time and had not eaten the marshmallow, he found that they were described as more competent in academic and social areas, better able to handle frustration and stress, better able to resist temptation, more successful in school, more harmonious in relationships, and less likely to be overweight.[26] In terms of all the criteria studied, they were more successful. Discipline pays off.

Roya Baumeister, a psychologist and author of the book "Willpower"[27] summarizes the benefits of strong self-control as follows:

> "The ability to regulate our impulses and desires is indispensable to success in living and working with others. People with good control over their thought processes, emotions and behaviors not only flourish in

school and in their jobs but are also healthier, wealthier and more popular. And they have better intimate relationships (as their partners confirm) and are more trusted by others. What is more, they are less likely to go astray by getting arrested, becoming addicted to drugs or experiencing unplanned pregnancies. They even live longer. Brazilian writer Paulo Coelho summed up these benefits in one of his novels: "If you conquer yourself, then you will conquer the world.""[28]

While discipline is genetic to a certain extent, it can also be developed to a great part. All it takes is a few simple things.

1. Set attractive goals and be sparing with discipline

There are not many researchers who have studied discipline more intensively than the social psychologist Roy Baumeister. He conducted a whole series of experiments to understand what constitutes discipline. He wanted to know why it is so difficult for some people to keep themselves under control while others find it very easy, and he investigated how discipline can be learned, etc. One of his key findings: Discipline is a finite resource. It can be compared to a muscle. Baumeister observed time and again that we find self-control particularly difficult when we are cognitively tired: The more participants strained their will, the more likely they were to succumb to the next temptation, especially if it occurred shortly thereafter.[29] In one of his experiments, participants were asked into a room where there were plates of warm cookies and chocolate, as well as plates of radishes. Half of the subjects were allowed to eat sweets, the other half only radishes. For many, this must have been a particularly mean test. The radish eaters gave up after eight minutes in a subsequent task - which was actually impossible to solve - while those who had been given sweets held out for 20 minutes.[30] Conclusion: The radish eaters already had to show a lot of discipline before the problem-solving task, they were already somewhat mentally exhausted and then didn't last long.

Discipline works a lot like a muscle.[31] The more you use it, the more it tires. If you want to lose weight and give up alcohol, stop smoking and reduce your TV consumption at the same time, it will be difficult. You very likely won't have enough discipline to do it all together. So think carefully about what goal you want to set and use your discipline sparingly. It is a valuable resource that you should not waste. Make sure the goals you set are SMART: Specific, Measurable, Attractive, Realistic and Timed. You need progress monitoring and a sense of accomplishment - even small progress can be motivating to persevere.

However, discipline, like a muscle, can also be trained. Research has shown that people who regularly practice discipline in one area become much better at developing this virtue and eventually develop more self-control and willpower in other areas of life as well.

2. Keep meticulous records of your achievements and progress

If you want to maintain your motivation to be disciplined, monitor yourself, and do so in a disciplined and regular manner! I kept a daily record of my training, comparing my volume and training success - measured, for example, by VO2 Max (maximum oxygen uptake) or FTP (functional threshold power, the maximum wattage over one hour) - with my goals and comparing my training workload with that of the previous month and the previous year. In this way, I recorded all my progress. This was an important motivating factor in all the years of training.

Anyone who has ever wanted to lose weight knows how important progress monitoring is for motivation. Researchers have found that people who want to reduce their weight are more likely to achieve their goals the more frequently they weigh themselves. Who controls its weight regularly, reaches its goals better, less often surrenders to the temptation of eating to much and is clearly less frustrated: The more carefully and more frequently you control yourselves, the better you have yourselves under control[32] - so simply is it. Even the most minimal forms of control work. Prison inmates have been found time and again to continuously gain weight. The reason: they don't wear belts or tight clothing, and in their loose overalls or wide pants they hardly notice that they are gaining weight. No waistband pinches, no belt has to be adjusted one hole further, etc.[33]

3. Formulate realization intentions

Vague intentions are usually ineffective. Therefore, formulate clear implementation intentions. My two-week training plans specified for each individual day the type of training (e.g., basic endurance, pace, V02 Max, active recovery workouts), the intensity of the training (e.g., how many intervals, how long they were, how much time should be between intervals), and the duration of the training. My training plans were specific and detailed. I always received them on Sunday evenings. Immediately, I checked them against my calendar and determined the times each day I wanted to implement the plan and the distances I would ride.

If you want to implement a plan successfully, you need very specific implementation intentions. Implementation intentions define exactly how, when and where you want to do something. Vague plans hardly get you to your goal. For example, in a study on breast cancer screening, researchers found that women who had realization intentions for their breast cancer self-exams completed them 100 percent of the time. Women who had the best intentions for self-examination, but did not make them specific, performed these exams only 53 percent of the time.[34] Another study came to a similar conclusion. As part of health programs, people were to be motivated to exercise regularly. Some of them were asked to formulate clear realization intentions (e.g., "Next week I will exercise intensively for at least 20 minutes on day XX at XX o'clock in XX (location)").

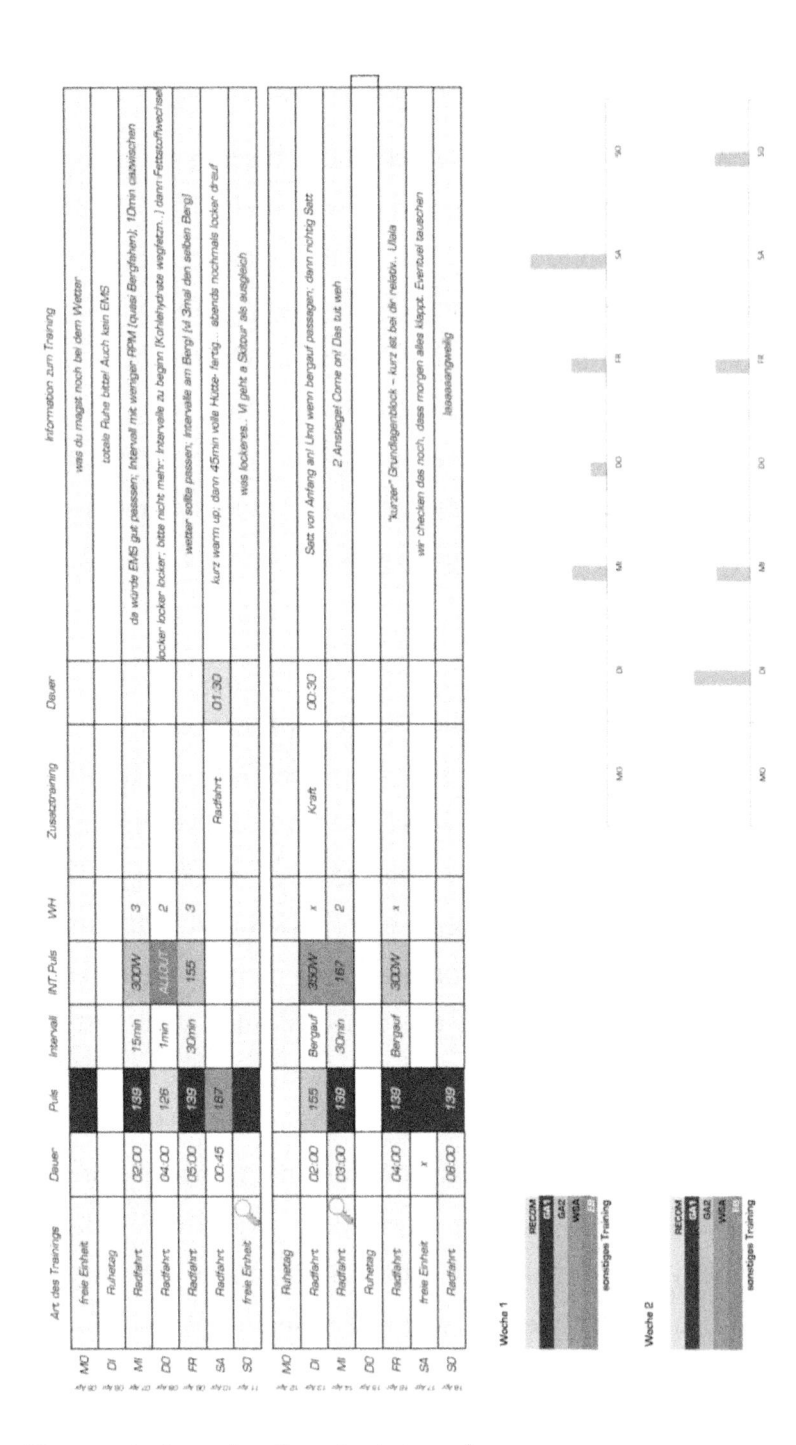

Two typical weeks of my training plan.

The others were simply told about the importance of regular exercise, and they stated their intentions to exercise in a motivated manner. While the former implemented their intention 100 percent of the time, only 40 percent of the second group actually exercised.[35] The road to hell is paved with good intentions. So develop very specific action plans if you want to be successful in implementing your intentions.

4. Make your commitment public

People have a strong need for consistency. It is important to them that their actions are in line with what they say. If we make a public commitment, we are much more likely to act accordingly afterwards. In one study, Israeli researchers report how they were very successful in getting residents of an apartment block to donate money for the construction of a rehabilitation center for the disabled. First, they asked some residents to simply sign a petition to build this rehabilitation center. This was a good thing and signing the petition was not a big effort. Just about everyone who was asked to sign supported the project. Two weeks later, the scientists now asked all residents of the building complex to donate to the project. Of those who were not previously asked to sign the petition, just half donated. But 92 percent of all those who had signed the petition gave a monetary contribution![36] How can this be explained? By signing the petition, they made something of a public commitment, and when asked to donate, they were not going to disagree. Their need for consistency prompted them to donate. Consistency needs can be very strong at times. We can observe this in ourselves over and over again. For example, when we take a stand in a discussion with others. Once we have positioned ourselves with an opinion, we try to stick with it. Even if we realize that we are wrong, we try to defend this position once it has been made public. Psychologist Robert Cialdini writes in his book "The Psychology of Persuasion": If one can get you to *commit* (i.e., to take a stand, to *commit to* something), he has created the conditions for you to act automatically and without much thought in accordance with that commitment. Once you have taken a stand, there is a natural inclination to remain consistent (or consistent) with that stand.[37]

Use this principle for your discipline. An experiment on a 16-week weight loss program for women in a fitness center examined the role of public commitment in goal achievement.[38] Participating women were divided into three groups. One group set a goal but made no public commitment to it. A second group publicly stated their long-term weight loss goal after 16 weeks: It was written on a card with the participant's name and posted on a bulletin board in the gym for all to see. A third group of women only posted a short-term goal (three weeks). Which group do you think was the most successful? Sure. The women who had publicly communicated their goal! At the conclusion of the entire program, participants were asked to step on the scale: Women who had published their long-term goal had a goal achievement of 103 percent; they actually lost slightly more weight than planned. Women who published their short-term goal achieved on average of 97 percent of their goal, and women who did not make a public commitment achieved only 89 percent of the goal.

So use a little trick to put a little more pressure on yourself. Make your goal public! Let others know what you want to achieve! Make a public commitment! Each year of our RAAM participation, we formulated a fundraising goal that we communicated publicly. This public commitment created the necessary pressure to push ourselves and give our all to reach that goal. In each year of our RAAM participation, our fundraising results exceeded our goal. Over $4.2 million was eventually raised in total!

5. Use the power of habit

"Discipline means: doing things you hate as if you loved them!" the boxer Mike Tyson once said. Discipline requires a lot of mental strength. If you have to think back and forth every time about whether or not to do something, you will quickly become exhausted and your morale will dwindle. The psychologist Roy Baumeister mentioned earlier calls this "ego exhaustion."[39] The good news, though, is that discipline is easy to learn. Create habits. If you always do things the same way in the same place at the same time, in other words, if you create routines, the constant decision-making falls away. Automatism develops. Without thinking long and hard, you just do things. This saves mental energy and helps you get where you want to go. This leads us to the next leadership lesson.

Leadership Lesson 2: Use the power of habit

What do Winston Churchill and Jennifer Aniston have in common? Winston Churchill, the British Prime Minister during World War II (and then again later), was known for his productivity. Actress Jennifer Aniston is admired for her flawless looks. No matter how different the two are, they have one thing in common. For both of them, their morning routines play an important role. Winston Churchill had an extremely structured workday:

> He woke up at 7:30 every day, took his breakfast in bed, read the newspapers, worked and dictated to his secretaries.
>
> At 11 o'clock he got up, took a walk in the garden and had a whiskey and soda.
>
> At 1 pm, he received guests and family for dinner.
>
> At 3:30 p.m., he was working in his study.
>
> At 5 p.m. he slept for an hour and a half, then took a bath and prepared for dinner.
>
> Before going to bed, he went back to his study for another hour.

Practically every day followed the same pattern, his habits determined the daily routine, and he rarely deviated from them.[40]

Jennifer Aniston, the actress, gets up at 4:30 a.m., drinks a cup of hot water with lemon, washes up, meditates, drinks a protein shake and then works out,[41] she walks her dogs, and - how interesting - she spends the first hour and a half of each day without a smartphone: "No phones, no email no texting and no social media. No looking at any of that for a good hour, hour and a half. I highly recommend doing a week of it, you won't believe the difference."[42]

Daily routines not only make our lives easier, they also ensure that we are more productive, don't waste our limited cognitive resources on mundane everyday decisions, and are more disciplined in working toward our goals. In a study of employees' daily morning routines, researchers examined how these habits affect workplace behavior.[43] They observed them over a three-week period and surveyed them several times a day. Employees who strictly followed their daily morning routines (e.g., breakfast, morning exercise, commuting to work, etc.) had more mental energy in their daily routines, reported more mental calmness, were more engaged at work, and achieved their goals better. If they deviated from their morning routines, they were less engaged, made less progress, were more mentally exhausted and less calm. The study authors attribute this to the higher cognitive effort that occurs when we deviate from habits. Have you ever wondered why we almost always eat the same thing for breakfast? Not only is it convenient, it's also very efficient. We all have limited cognitive energy, and if we already have to use it for mundane everyday decisions, we have less energy left for work.

Habits play a big role for me. In the beginning, I very often found it very difficult to fulfill my training workload. I came home at irregular times in the evening, was usually tired and often downright exhausted. I was hungry, ate something, and while I was still eating, a battle began in my head: "Should I train now? Maybe I'd better postpone it until tomorrow, or do a slightly shorter training session and do a little more tomorrow?" At some point I had enough of it and changed my rhythm. I moved my daily training to the morning. It was much easier for me then. I got up early, had a light breakfast and got on my indoor bike. Soon it became a habit and followed an automatic pattern. I no longer thought about whether or not I should exercise now - I just did it. No more permanent thinking, no more guilty conscience, no more procrastination. I found it much easier to achieve my workout workload during the week. Daily routines make our lives more pleasant and efficient in many ways. Discipline is no longer difficult, and we use a scarce resource - our mental energy - sparingly. Used correctly, habits determine success and failure. The founder of the body therapy named after him, F. M. Alexander, put it in a nutshell: "People do not decide about their future. They decide about their habits, and these habits determine the future!"

So create routines for tasks that are important to you, require a lot of discipline, and are otherwise difficult to do for you. In doing so, consider three things:

1. Make sure you set a specific time slot and place for these activities. If there are a few things that you don't like to do at all, that you keep putting off or just keep forgetting about, then set a day, time and place to devote to those tasks. Make sure there are no distractions. For example, Friday afternoons are great for those pesky office chores. Make it a habit to always do these tasks at the same time in the same place. With this routine, not only will you have these chores done on a regular basis, you will also create a small sense of accomplishment and a pleasant feeling for the weekend.
2. Tie these activities to specific events. For example, if you resolve to drink more water, link this intention to an event: "Every time I go to a meeting, I take a bottle of water with me" or "Every time I drink a coffee, I take a glass of water with me". If you want to walk more steps, forgo the elevator. If you want to sit less and stand more at the office, attend Zoom meetings standing. Make a habit of it. These are very small, trivial-seeming things, but they help us develop routines and make our lives better in many small - and often big - ways.
3. Repeat these activities regularly. Only through repetition does the habit develop. "Habit formation is the process by which a behaviour becomes progressively more automatic through repetition. The more you repeat an activity, the more the structure of your brain changes to become efficient at that activity.[44] explains James Clear in his book "Atomic Habits." In fact, scientists have found in studies that brain structures change. Musicians have a

larger cerebellum, responsible for physical processes like plucking a guitar string, than non-musicians. Cab drivers in London have a larger hippocampus - responsible for spatial memory.

Leadership Lesson 3: Always try in all things to combine what is pleasing to yourself with what is useful to others

This wisdom of Hodja Nasreddin[45] was the guiding principle of our entire Race Across America project. We combined our passion for road cycling with a fundraising project. Our motto "We ride so that others can walk" expressed this.

When we manage to combine different things in such a way, we not only add value to our activities, we use our time twice! I applied this simple principle to my training as well. My morning routine of working out on the indoor bike included doing my reading work for the office. In the office, I gathered material that I could read well during low heart rate workouts. This included textbooks, academic journals, case studies for my classes as well as newspaper articles. My workouts on the roller always followed the same pattern: first I read the newspaper, then a scientific article, and then at least one chapter from a book. During longer training sessions, I listened to podcasts and audio books. I watched YouTube videos and educated myself in this way during training. This became my daily morning routine. When I got to the office around 9 a.m. - often the same time as my colleagues - there was a difference: I had already worked out for one to two hours and worked for one to two hours. So while I was working out, I was reading thousands of pages a year and listening to countless podcasts and audiobooks. What surprises many is that the years since my first Race Across America participation were the most productive years in my career. During this period, I published over 30 papers in scientific journals and several books. Some of my most important work came out of this period, including our book, Open Strategy (MIT Press, 2021), which was named the best strategy book of the year by Business+Strategy magazine and was nominated for the Thinkers50 Strategy Award - an award given every two years for the best management ideas in the world. It is among the best leadership books (LeadershipBlog) and among the best management books of the year (The Globe and Mail), and it received the international Axiom Award (Bronze). All of this scholarly publishing activity requires a great deal of reading, and I'm sure that my reading load far exceeds that of most other scholars because of my training.

Our time is limited. But if we use it according to the motto "Always combine the pleasant with the useful", we can get much more out of it.

Off to the desert

Ten days before the start, I set off for California with my crew chief Zoltàn Bogdàn for heat acclimatization in the desert. The days before, I had still taken care of logistical things. About 300 kilograms of luggage had to be brought to the USA - four bikes, about 50 kilograms of liquid food, a few kilograms of beverage powder for my sports drinks, tools, spare parts, clothing, etc. Originally, I was only going to take three bikes: my time trial bike for the flat stages, my Tarmac SL7 with Alpinist wheels for the mountains, and my S-Works Venge with aerobars as an all-around bike. Three weeks before departure, however, I decided to additionally pack my old S-Works Venge 2015. The bike had been to RAAM four times, the Race Around Austria twice and the Race Across Italy once. The Race Across America is unpredictable. A lot can happen on the 5000 kilometers under the most difficult conditions. Again and again we had major defects with the bikes, so I thought to myself: plan for the worst, hope for the best. My cycling teammate Didi lent me an extra bike case. It was a good decision, as it turned out on the second day of the race.

Once we arrived in Los Angeles, we headed to Palm Springs in a rental car. There it was hot enough for my heat acclimatization. Daily training sessions at 45 to 50 degrees Celsius prepared me well for the heat. Heat acclimatization is an important part of preparation: "The organism can acclimate to heat in 5 to 10 days, when the core body temperature rises to 40°C during training. Acclimatization triggered by heat training is characterized by lowered core body temperature, lowered salinity in sweat, decreasing heart rate, and increase in plasma volume and sweat formation rate,"[46] I read in a journal article. By exercising daily for about two hours, bringing the core body temperature above 39 degrees, the body begins to adapt. I exercised at the hottest time of the day - over lunch. Two hours at up to 50 degrees at 250 watts, with 400-watt intervals of five minutes each in between. According to Garmin, which displays the heat acclimatization, the training was probably effective; I was already at 100 percent after six days.

Heat acclimatization in the desert near Palm Springs. (Photo: Kurt Matzler)

Zoli accompanied me during the training in the desert. To ride alone would have been too big a risk. I trained on the time trial bike, Zoli rode my three-month-old Tarmac SL7. On the second day, a loop of about 60 kilometers was on the agenda. I rode ahead, Zoli in my slipstream. On the way back, I noticed that I was suddenly alone. I looked back and saw Zoli standing a few hundred meters behind me. He was gesticulating wildly, and I immediately realized he had a problem. The freewheel on his bike was broken, he was just freaking out. We were lucky, it was no more than a kilometer or two to the next gas station. I was able to push him until then and then pick him up there by car. I can't imagine if that had happened an hour further out in the middle of the desert at 50 degrees or even during the race!

We found a small workshop that could solve the problem with the spring in the freewheel and were optimistic that it was done. We were wrong, another defect occurred. Now we looked for help in a special store. There they were able to fix the damage, and as luck would have it, we met Leah Goldstein there, the RAAM winner from the previous year. Due to the Corona restrictions, almost only Americans had been able to participate in 2021. The starting field was very small with twelve participants, and only three finished due to the extreme heat. The race went down in history as one of the toughest. Leah Goldstein was the first woman to win RAAM as the overall winner at eleven days, three hours and three minutes. We talked for a while, said our goodbyes, and saw each other again in Oceanside - Leah was racing the Race Across the West that year, a leg of RAAM from Oceanside to Durango in Colorado.

After a few days of heat training, Zoli and I headed back to Los Angeles. We picked up Ruth and Balázs. Zoli and Balázs went on to Oceanside, for Ruth and me there were two more days in the desert in Borrego Springs. Borrego Springs is located on the RAAM course, it is the first town to be reached on the evening of the first day of the race. This makes it a popular destination among RAAM participants for heat acclimation, and indeed we met a few colleagues there. I completed a few training rides and relaxed by the pool at our hotel. There I also met Rainer Steinberger, who was considered the absolute favorite for the race. The likeable ultracyclist from the Bavarian Forest could boast some victories, among others at the Race Around Austria, the Race Across Germany and the Glocknerman. We were glad to escape the hustle and bustle of Oceanside for a few more days and enjoyed the peace and quiet. We talked about the race, race strategies and all sorts of things. I let him know that it was clear to me that he would win this race.

He just said, "Possibly, if I finish at all."

A gloomy premonition that this time it might not end well for him.

On Saturday, June 11, Ruth and I finally made our way to Oceanside, where the race would start on Tuesday. Darlene and Bob, Zoli and Balázs were already there and had already started the first preparations. The rented cars had to be stickered, lights had to be mounted according to the specifications, speakers had to be installed, navigation had to be prepared, reflectors had to be attached to the wheels, shopping had to be done, etc.

My crew was very creative in designing the support vehicles, each was given its own name and designed accordingly:

RAAMbulance: Ruth, Alex and Liane. This car, with the team doctor, a pharmacist and a biologist, was mainly responsible for my health and physical well-being.

RAAMbler: Zoli, Florian and Balázs. This trio with crew chief Zoli took over the night shift.

RAAMerica: Bob, Darlene and Bill. The three Americans were assigned to the first shift after the sleep break.

RAAMedia: Hubert, Martin and Roland. The media vehicle that was responsible for filming for TV station K19 and for press relations.

In addition, there were a few mandatory meetings (official photo session, crew chief meeting, submission of race documents, etc.). Just like in 2019, we were invited to the official press conference. I sat next to Rainer Steinberger and Elin Starup from Denmark. She had failed in her first RAAM attempt and was full of optimism that it would work out this year. After 550 miles, however, her dream was shattered. She came to a crash, and with a fracture of her finger, her race was over. Together with her team, she then drove the entire distance in the car and kept showing up to motivate the race participants. Rainer Steinberger also did not finish the race. While in the lead, he had a serious crash in the Rocky Mountains and spent some time in hospital with serious injuries.

Saturday, June 11	12:20	• Darlene picks up the race packet / Harbor Lot 498-100 Riverside Drive • Crew puts signage on the vehicles / hotel parking lot • Self-inspections of vehicles and bicycles / hotel parking lot
Sunday, June 12	11:00 12:30-2:30	• Photos / Harbor Lot 498-100 Riverside Drive • Jersey sizing (Kurt) / Harbor Lot 498-100 Riverside Drive • Crew Chief Meeting (Zoli & Darlene) Library / 330 N Coast Hwy. • Darlene TURN IN BINDER
Monday, June 13	10:00-12:00 11:30-12:30 5:00-6:30	• Cargo drop off / Harbor Lot 498-100 Riverside Drive • Media Crew Meeting (Roland & Martin) / Library / 330 N Coast Hwy • Racer Meeting (MANDATORY) Community Bldg. 300 The Strand N

Race preparations in Oceanside.

After the press conference we walked towards the sea and found a nice restaurant where we had lunch. Martin had a small Bluetooth speaker with him, which he put on the table after the meal and played a song. What a surprise! With his friend Markus Linder, a well-known Tyrolean cabaret artist and bluesman, he had rewritten the song "Route 66" by Nat King Cole and sung and recorded it for me. Our RAAM song was born!

Route RAAM

If you ever plan to bike the RAAM
join Kurt Matzler on his ride, an incredible man
He keeps his pace on the world's toughest bicycle race

It winds more than 3000 miles all the way
through burning deserts, up steep mountains, night and day
He keeps his pace on the world's toughest bicycle race.

Well you go through Alamosa and Jefferson City and
Bloomington, Indiana, is mighty pretty.
You'll see Montezuma and El Dorado, Kansas,
Navajo Reservation, the Rockies of the Nation,
Greensburg, Oxford, Mississippi River ...

Won't you get hip to this timely tip
when THAT Kurt takes that big American trip
He'll keep his pace on the world's toughest bicycle race.

Well you go through Alamosa and Jefferson City and
Bloomington, Indiana, is so mighty pretty.
You'll see Montezuma and El Dorado, Kansas,
Navajo Reservation, the Rockies of the Nation,
Greensburg, Oxford, Mississippi River ...

Won't you get hip to this timely tip
when OUR Kurt takes that big American trip
He'll keep his pace on the world's toughest bicycle race.

To avoid the hectic pace before the race, I tried to stay out of the preparations as much as possible. My crew took care of everything, and there was an agreement that no problem would be brought to my attention - at least not until there was a solution to it.

And indeed, in the last days before the race, a few major problems emerged that I didn't hear about at first. Hubert, Martin, Florian and Roland flew from Munich to San Diego on Saturday, June 11. Zoli picked them up from the airport in the evening, but only three had arrived. Hubert had a problem with his ESTA (travel authorization) at the airport in Munich. He had applied for it and received it, but at the airport he was denied check-in: since he had received a new passport after applying for the ESTA, it was no longer valid. Roland, Martin and Florian had to fly without him. Somehow, however, he managed to get a new ESTA and a flight a few hours later within a very short time - even without a rebooking fee. Our big fundraising project had probably been convincing enough in the discussions with Lufthansa.

But that was not to be the only travel problem. Alexandra, my doctor, wanted to join us on Monday evening - one day before the start. She had another event in Austria over the weekend and could not fly earlier. On Sunday, she received word that her flight was ready to board - due to a booking error, her flight was booked for Sunday, not Monday! She panicked slightly. There was no way she could catch the flight; she would never have made it to Munich on time. At the last moment, she managed to get a flight on Monday to join the already almost complete team in the USA in time.

Liane was booked on a flight from Amsterdam to San Diego on June 14. She was to arrive there a few hours after take-off and be picked up by Ruth and Alex. This was hardly a detour for them, as they were traveling from Oceanside to Brawley. The airport is more or less on that route. At Brawley, their first shift was scheduled to begin at 4:50 a.m. Wednesday. Liane started for the airport five hours before departure on Monday, but was horrified to discover that passengers were already lined up for check-in well outside the airport terminal. Due to staffing problems, there was absolute chaos. Liane realized that there would never be enough time to get to the gate on time. Her husband helped her smuggle her over a barrier. In tears, she explained to the airport employee what was at stake. That helped - Liane was pushed ahead and reached the plane at the last minute. It's hard to imagine if Hubert, Alex and Liane hadn't made it!

Something always goes wrong at RAAM, and we were convinced that we had already had our share of bad luck. From now on, no more problems - at least we hoped!

Until the day of the start, I was extremely relaxed and calm. However, when I woke up on Race Day, I felt an incredible nervousness. My pulse rate was much higher and I was very tense. While my crew was still making the final preparations, I stayed in my hotel room, watched "Forrest Gump" to relax and glanced at the clock every five minutes. In a few hours we were off.

Race Across America 2022

The start

The emotions at the start of this race are indescribable. You stand at the starting line and know that you now have 5,000 kilometers and over 40,000 meters of climbing ahead of you, up to 50 degrees Celsius in the desert, the Rocky Mountains, the endless straights of the Great Plains. Wind, sun, rain, cold, sleep deprivation, pain and total exhaustion. But also indescribable moments of happiness, unique landscape experiences and fun with the team. You have no idea what all is in store for you. Will the weather be ok? What technical problems will arise? Will my body be strong enough? Will everything work with the crew and the vehicles?

Race Across America 2022 – Race Roster

Solos

268	Ricardo Arap - BRA		642	Paolo Pietro Godardi – ITA
300	Jim Trout - USA		644	Peter Trachsel - SUI
399	Valerio Zamboni – MON		645	Rainer Steinberger - DEU
448	Srinivas Gokulnath - IND		647	Rupert Guinness – AUS
455	Svata Bozak - CZE		650	Vivek Shah - IND
539	Kari Rouvinen - FIN		654	Kurt Matzler - AUS
549	Nicole Reist - SUI		655	Martin Neitzke – GER
599	Christian Mauduit - FRA		658	Phil Fox - USA
608	Elin Starup - DEN		659	Simon Potter – GBR
610	Kabir Rachure - IND		660	Soren Peter Rosenkilde – DEN
620	Allan Jefferson - AUS		661	Sebastien Sasseville - CAN
624	Bharat Pannu – IND		663	Guy Stapleford – GBR
625	Dorina Vaccaroni – USA		664	Adriano Ongaro – ITA
627	Graham Macken – IRL		665	Les Crooks – USA
628	James Golding – GBR		668	Peter Skovbak – DEN
632	Joff Spencer Jones – GBR		670	Jean-Luc Perez – FRA
634	Chris Davies – USA		671	Arvis Sprude – LVA
635	Lionel Poggio – SUI			

Race Across America 2022 start list.

At 1:05 p.m. I set off. I had planned my first stage with 551 kilometers and 3400 meters of climbing to Salome in Arizona. With an average speed of 22.5 km/h I should go into my first sleep break after about 24 hours. The first miles are neutralized and follow a bike path out of town. The actual race starts after 16 miles at Old Castle Road, from there on support vehicles are allowed. The 20 degrees in Oceanside soon became 35 to 40 degrees inland. The first 120 kilometers to the so-called Glass Elevator, a nine-mile long descent that leads over 1200 meters of altitude down into the desert, had it all. A permanent up and down with many steep climbs - the Sleeping Indian has a gradient of 16 percent. I tried to ride in a controlled manner to conserve my energy, paying attention to my heart rate and watts. Soon I was being passed by other racers. I began to have doubts about my fitness. How could it be that so many were passing me? It was frustrating. After a while, though, I noticed that most were riding very unrhythmically. In their euphoria after the start, they competed on every climb and delivered one attack after another. It almost seemed as if they were pushing themselves to the limit. A suspicion that was confirmed - towards the end of the climb, most of them were again pushed to the back of the pack. The unreasonable and reckless race behavior of some participants let me already suspect at the Glass Elevator who would make it to the finish and who would not. In Annapolis I had a conversation with one of these riders. We happened to be in the same hotel, and he told me that he had felt incredibly strong on the first day. He had felt so good that he rode the first hills with a heart rae of up to 180 bpm! You don't need to be a competitive athlete to know that's anything but reasonable. You can't win RAAM on the first mountains - you can only lose it there. It's quite crucial to ride consistently and with a low intensity. I don't know whether this was due to a lack of experience, recklessness or the euphoria on the first day of the race - in any case, some people wasted a lot of energy on the first day.

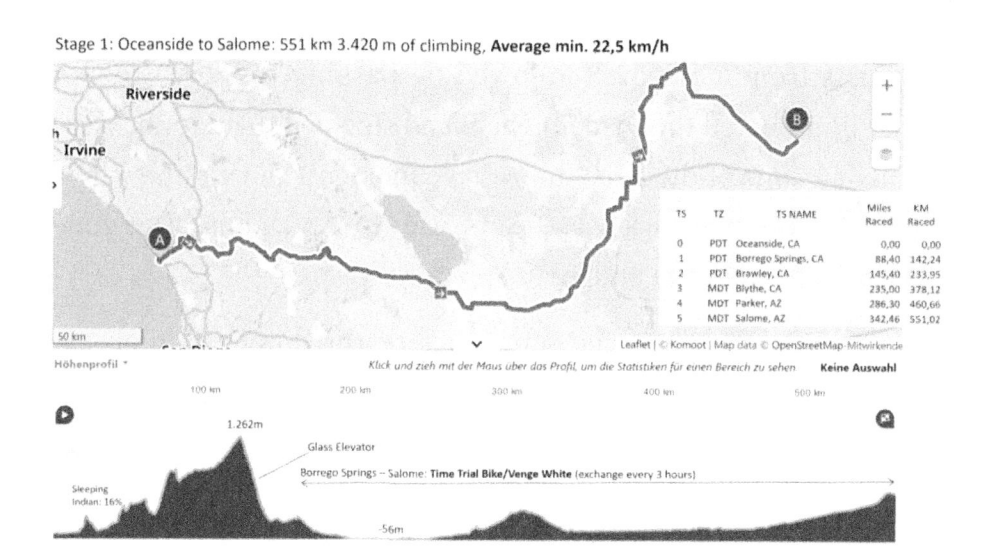

RAAM - the first stage.

So on the Glass Elevator it was clear to me that I was relatively far behind. That didn't irritate me any further. I rode my race for me and my goal and didn't want to be distracted and certainly not from my strategy. The descent into the desert was by far not as dangerous as expected, the gusty crosswinds were absent. There are always crashes on this stretch. The race can be over here after just a few hours if you are not careful enough.

The YouTube video of Stefan Schlegel's crash in 2014 is probably familiar to every RAAM participant as an example.

With every meter of altitude down, I now noticed how it was getting hotter. In Borrego Springs, 45 degrees were waiting for me. I got on the time trial bike and continued to ride at a controlled pace, but noticed that I was overtaking more and more competitors. The night under the full moon in the desert was an unforgettable experience. You could see the other cyclists from a distance, followed by flashing support vehicles that illuminated the road for them and shielded them to the rear. This was one of the most impressive moments during the whole race. The entire pack was on its way to Annapolis. Everyone was full of euphoria and good spirits.

Slowly, a certain routine set in. Every three hours I took my five-minute break, was well looked after by my crew and I reached my first hotel in Salome after 21.5 hours - almost three hours faster than planned. At the time station Salome, I was in fourth place. But I didn't know that at that time - I wanted to do my race for myself and had agreed with my crew that I was not to be told anything about ranks and intermediate results. I wanted to stick to my strategy, unaffected by anything that was happening around me.

A support vehicle had already checked into the hotel and was waiting for me. I immediately took a sleeping pill, took a shower, was examined by my doctor and massaged to sleep by Zoli and Alex. We had agreed that - should I be faster than planned - the time credit would be invested in additional sleep. After about two hours, however, I woke up and went outside, where almost the entire crew was gathered.

"Let's move on," I shouted, looking at astonished faces.

No one had probably expected me to wake up so early on my own. Since I felt very well rested, I insisted on starting. Zoli was not entirely convinced, but he agreed.

> "The sleep break is over. The crew wanted to let him sleep longer, Kurt wanted to get on his bike. So we soaked his jersey and bandana in ice water, applied double sunscreen and put *crushed ice in* his water bottle. So we sent him on the track at 45 degrees Celsius. There are now 419 km and 5300 meters of climbing ahead of him until the next sleep break" wrote Martin and Florian in the race diary on www.radsport-news.com.

A long day in the sweltering Arizona heat awaited me.

Day 2 - The big heat

Since the first stage with 551 kilometers through the desert was very exhausting, I planned the second stage a little shorter: 419 kilometers and over 5000 meters of climbing to Flagstaff. At first it was still flat, so I started on the time trial bike. Bob, Darlene and Bill accompanied me for the first eight hours, the night shift was done by Zoli, Florian and Balázs. Ruth, Alex and Liane were responsible for the last hours until the sleep break. The afternoon was blisteringly hot: we measured 51 degrees

Celsius as the maximum temperature. Now we had to pull out all the stops: Dehydration and heat stroke had to be avoided at all costs. The heat also radiated off the road asphalt, which can easily heat up to 95 degrees Celsius here. If the cyclist falls, the crew has to be quick and get him off the road immediately. Time and again, there are reports of people - often homeless people - suffering terrible burn injuries on the asphalt in the desert.

The acclimatization in the desert before the race had paid off. But what was coming up now was another level higher and reached the limits of human endurance. After only two hours of sleep, I left the chilled room and got on my bike. I had the feeling that the heat would crush me. Not even the breeze cooled down. On the contrary - the hot air blew into my face as if from a hairdryer, and it was almost painful to breathe. In Palm Springs I had gotten myself insulated drinking bottles, I got a 750-milliliter bottle of ice-cold, isotonic drink about every 45 minutes. That works out to 20 liters per day. My crew monitored me constantly, watching for any signs of dehydration such as chapped, cracked lips, dry skin, lack of concentration and the color of my urine. At the same time, however, my team was not allowed to give in to my constant urging for more to drink. If the body is flooded with water, it can have fatal health consequences, as can dehydration. Excess fluid intake causes an influx of water into the cells and leads to a drop in blood salt levels. The consequences range from mild swelling of the legs or hands to lung edema, cramps or even death.

Therefore, in order to detect weight fluctuations at an early stage, not only my fluid intake and excretions were monitored, but also my body weight - I also got on the scale after each sleep break.

Managing water balance is complex and should be familiar to an ultra-endurance athlete. Again and again, however, you encounter participants with swollen legs and arms, cyclists with swollen faces, and even some who have to cut open the front of their cycling shoes because their swollen feet no longer fit into them. My crew was therefore instructed to pay particular attention to my calf muscles - as long as you could see the tendons and veins and the contours of the muscles clearly, I was allowed to continue following my drinking plan.

Christoph Strasser also had to experience that this issue can be very dangerous at the Race Across America 2015. It was extremely hot in the desert this year, and Christoph had probably drunk too much: "Anyway, I had problems with hydration since the second day, my face was puffy and my weight increased. I looked like one of those Michelin men - except I wasn't smiling," he writes in his book "Strasser's Road"[47] These water deposits can then become particularly dangerous at altitude. The route of the RAAM leads the athletes after the desert into the Rocky Mountains and thus to over 3,000 meters in altitude. If pulmonary edema develops, pneumonia is almost inevitable, and Christoph Strasser was not spared. Already during the ascents in the Rocky Mountains, he noticed that something was wrong. He managed the passes with last efforts. But on the Cucharas Pass, the last in the Rocky Mountains, his doctor diagnosed bronchitis, which had developed from the pulmonary edema. Strasser had to get to lower elevations as quickly as possible. But it was already too late for a successful finish, the multiple RAAM winner had to end the race in Kansas. The Styrian had also had a similar experience in 2009, back then he even ended up in intensive care. But we were allowed to learn a lot from these lessons, in an episode of his podcast "Sitzfleisch" fluid management is discussed in detail. Above all, my doctor made sure that I took just the right amount of fluid. It was a fine balancing act. Time and again, I would go almost insane with thirst but not get anything to drink. I had already drunk too much and had to suffer. That was very hard, but it was important.

Any athlete with RAAM on their agenda should consider not only the significant physical stresses involved, but also their fluid balance. To illustrate the importance, here are a few interesting facts: The human body is made up of 50 to 80 percent water and about 4.5 to 6 liters of blood for an adult human. Blood is about 90 percent water and supplies all organs, especially the brain and muscles, with nutrients and oxygen. Accordingly, both too little and too much fluid intake can have a negative effect and pose a health risk.

If not enough fluid is supplied, this can have serious consequences for the organism. In the event of a water deficiency, the total volume of blood plasma decreases, as a result of which the flow properties of the blood deteriorate, the central blood volume and the stroke volume of the heart are reduced. Heart rate increases, while skin blood flow and sweating decrease. As a result, core body temperature rises. Sure signs of a water deficiency are dark urine because urine production decreases, and dry mouth due to reduced saliva production. Overall, a lack of fluids impairs both physical and mental performance. From a fluid loss of two to four percent of body weight, restrictions in strength and endurance performance are to be expected. Decreased cerebral blood flow due to even greater dehydration can lead to symptoms such as fatigue, headaches, concentration problems and prolonged reaction times, and ultimately increase the risk of heat-related consequences such as heat cramps, heat exhaustion and heat stroke. So one might conclude that drinking enough would be beneficial - especially when it's up to 50 degrees Celsius in the Arizona desert. However, it is much less well known that excessive fluid intake also increases the risk of hyponatremia (water intoxication), which in extreme cases has also led to deaths among recreational athletes (triathletes and marathon runners). Heavy sweating leads not only to increased water loss but also to a strong loss of salt, especially sodium. Excessive intake of mineral-poor water leads to hyperhydration with hyponatremia, simply put, water accumulation in the tissues, especially the lungs and brain. Breathing problems, pneumonia, headaches and impaired consciousness are the result. For the alpinists among you, it is worth mentioning the ascent to over 3000 meters altitude in the Rocky Mountains that follows the desert. The risk of high-altitude pulmonary edema is of course much higher if fluid management is unsuccessful.

We were well prepared for the heat in everything: I had white cycling shorts, white shoes, white gloves, white sleeves, heat-insulated water bottles, cooling towels and even a special cooling liquid to soak my jersey in. An application from emergency medicine - mixing this cooling liquid with water and contact with the air immediately produces a strong cooling effect that lasts one to two hours. My jersey, sleeves and headgear were dipped in it. The cooling effect did not last for two hours at 50 degrees Celsius, but it was enough for 20 to 30 minutes anyway. Putting it on took a lot of effort - the jersey was so ice-cold that the first touch almost hurt, a video recording shows me gasping for air with a pain-distorted face due to the cold shock.

The heat in the desert was joined by extreme dryness. Again and again I was sprayed with cold water. For a few seconds this provided relief, but within a very short time I was dry again. Even my sweat evaporated immediately, leaving salt crusts on my jersey. This dryness was especially a problem for the mucous membranes. In reports of former RAAM participants is to be read of drying out the mucous membranes up to pulmonary hemorrhages and infections of the respiratory tract.[48] Therefore, we had also dealt with this in the preparation and developed a protocol for the supply in the desert:

- Drinks with ice cubes
- Have 1 cool west in cooler
- Have 1 jersey in water with cool down fluid
- Have 1 cooling towel water with cool down fluid
- Have 1 pair of white arm sleeves water with cool down fluid
- Have 1 white bandana water with cool down fluid

- Spray cold water on head, cool west, or jersey (never on the bibs, pads must not be soaked with water)
- Important: white shoes, white bibs, white helmet, white arm sleeves and white gloves
- Coldamaris pastilles to suck every three hours
- Sun lotion
- Eyedrops
- Coldamaris nosespray

At every break there was already a camping chair and a parasol ready for me - thanks to my crew. Every single minute was used for my care: Food, drink, massage, catering. Here I could see a decisive difference to some other RAAM participants. I could often see my fellow racers taking breaks, standing in front of the car with their bikes - bent over the handlebars, heads down, the crew standing idly by. Not exactly a break that could be called productive. We didn't have anything like that. Every minute was used. Sometimes I tried to negotiate a few more minutes off, but especially in the first few days, my team stood firm for my sake.

So we had the heat under control. But the second day of the race was still to be one of the most difficult. We took a short break before Yarnell Grade, a 600-meter climb in the desert. I changed into a chilled jersey and switched to the Tarmac. The 40+ degree Celsius climb was easier than expected. I could actually really enjoy the landscape, the atmosphere and the race. My media team with Hubert, Roland and Martin were with me, filming and taking pictures.

After Yarnell Grade, short flat stages alternated with shorter climbs and descents, and at the next break I switched to my Venge. As I set off, I felt that the gears were not working. Had my crew perhaps forgotten to charge the battery? A quick check, no, it wasn't the battery. I stopped, Zoli jumped out of the support vehicle, ran to me and asked what was wrong. I only answered that the bike was broken. Zoli and Balázs, both good bike mechanics, were at a loss. Zoli concluded that it could only be the cable connection of the electronic gear shift. He assumed that the plug-in connection of the cables, which is routed inside the frame, had come loose - perhaps due to the vibrations on the bike rack during the car ride. This diagnosis later proved to be correct. The problem, however, was that it was necessary to disassemble the whole bike to fix the problem. So we needed a suitable workshop. This realization hit me like a bolt of lightning, as the Venge was my most important bike. Besides the time trial bike, it was the only one with aerobars, i.e. the only one to be used for long stages. But there was nothing we could do. Balázs prepared my Tarmac, I got on and continued. I remembered my carpal tunnel syndrome, which I had suffered from during the Race Across Italy and the Race Around Austria. Without the aerobars, the constant pressure on the palms would pinch off the nerves and soon numbness would set in. I wanted to avoid that at all costs.

In Prescott, Arizona the next shift change of the escort crew was scheduled. There I had a 15-minute break. It had already become dark. I asked Balázs to re-mount the Venge's aerobars onto the Tarmac. They didn't actually fit this stem, but somehow Balázs managed a reasonably wobbly construction with enough rubber under the clamps. But the riding and steering felt spongy. In any case, this compromise was better than riding without aerobars. The race could go on, and I was already looking forward to my next sleep break. Bob and his crew took care of the broken Venge, as Bob recounted: "Our crew had the bike after the shifting problem. We had spent the night in Prescott, AZ and I took it to a bike shop the first thing in the morning. They had an electronic detecting device that they hooked up and determined where the problem was. They then spent four hours taking the bike apart (even the bottom bracket) to try to get to the area. However, they did not have the replacement parts in stock and we needed to leave to catch you and do our shift. So, they put the bike back together and we were on our way. I then called my bike store in Tulsa and discussed the problem with Jake, the owner, and he directed us to the shop in Durango."

We had booked a hotel in Flagstaff, where I was to have a two-hour sleep break. For the next day, a 450-kilometer stage to Cortez in Colorado was planned. On the way to Flagstaff I realized that something was wrong. My crew was nervous, constantly on the phone, and I had the feeling that they were hiding something from me. It was already getting light again when I learned what had happened. Due to extensive forest fires near Flagstaff, the race organizers had decided on a detour - far away from our hotel. Driving on in these forest fires would simply have been too dangerous.

"Where do we take my sleep break?", I asked Zoli.

Winslow, a town of 9000 people in Navajo County in the US state of Arizona was on the detour, but a room was not available there. Zoli informed me about his decision: We had just got hold of a single room in Tuba City. There I could take my sleep break. The 420 kilometer stage turned into 600 kilometers with 6000 meters of climbing. Although we were allowed to be transported in the car for a small part of the detour, my stage was still much more than 100 kilometers longer than planned. In the end, a 19-hour stage turned into 27 hours. I was devastated when I learned what was immediately ahead of me. But Zoli was convinced of my physical and mental strength. He knew my performance levels, and he knew me. The next day's stage was going to be a little shorter for that. For the reroute, we received route descriptions at short notice - but so imprecisely that one could hardly estimate the actual altitude meters. In fact, the climbs were much longer than expected. That increasingly wore me down.

I had no choice, I had to go on. In Winslow, Ruth, Liane and Alex had been waiting for us for hours. They took over the escort from here to Tuba City. Around noon I arrived at their place and took a short power nap in the car. I had been on the road for about 20 hours, it was extremely hot, and there were still about 200 kilometers to the hotel. The route was now through the Hopi Indian Reservation. Since there was no phone or internet connection there, we were cut off from the outside world for a few hours. We had no information about the elevation profile of the detour and no idea what would be coming. Constant ups and downs, more and more elevation gain, and the route dragged on forever. I rode my Tarmac, and the support vehicle carried the time trial bike. Near Shongopovi, before a shorter climb, I saw our media team. It was standing on the side of the road and was busy recording. That was a highlight for me every time. Hubert, Martin and Roland were always in the best of moods, and of course the presence of a camera also pushed me to ride a bit more motivated. I passed them pushing the pedals very hard and didn't let the effort show. It was not far to the end of the hill. After that, another nice downhill was waiting for me. But I didn't get that far. On the last meters of the climb I recognized another racer in front of me. He was going very slowly and it was easy to overtake him. At the exact moment we were level, I suddenly stepped into the void. The freewheel!

"I don't believe it!" I yelled. I got off the bike, pushed the bike onto the side and sat down on the guardrails in frustration. The second defect in one day. And another one we couldn't fix ourselves. My brand-new Tarmac SL7 was only three months old, and on the second day of racing we were again faced with the same defect we had already had in the desert. Now it was getting serious. I only had the time trial bike left, and the remaining 100 kilometers to Tuba City were a constant up and down. With the time trial bike it was only possible with enormous effort - if at all. We had no telephone connection and no Internet. We were left to our own devices.

But there was still our media team, which had overtaken us a few minutes before the defect and was driving to Tuba City. They were waiting at a scenically exposed spot to take some last shots of me in the beginning sunset. After I didn't show up for some time, they decided to head back to check on me and the support vehicle. Not far from where they had passed us about 30 minutes earlier, they found us sitting quite distressed on the side of the road. Hubert jumped out of the car and asked what was wrong. He thought I had crashed. What a luck that the three of them showed up just at that moment! Three weeks before departure, I had decided to take my old Venge (2015) as a fourth bike - plan for the worst, hope for the best! I never thought we would need it at some point. Therefore, we had packed it into the media vehicle, because there was still enough space.

In Oceanside I had still said to Hubert, "Here we pack it in, and in Annapolis we unpack it again!"

The old Venge I had prepared for the Race Around Austria for the steep climbs, with compact crankset and 34r sprockets rear. Now this was my salvation. With this bike I could make it to Tuba City. If the media vehicle hadn't turned around, the whole race would have been on jeopardy. I might not have made the cut-off in Durango. The guys got the bike out of the car, quickly assembled it and put me on it.

"How can you have such bad luck?", I muttered in frustration.

Hubert had the right answer: "We don't have time to complain now! Keep riding! You have to make the cut-off!"

That was effective.

The remaining 100 kilometers can be described in one word "brutal". I had been on the bike for well over 20 hours, it was hot, and behind every climb there was another one waiting. At some point I was just desperate, even the girls in the support vehicle didn't really know how to motivate me anymore. Stomach cramps came along and I had to stop more often. After another two or three hours, I calculated that it could only be about ten miles to Tuba City, but again there was a long climb ahead of me. I struggled to get to the top. Once there, I surveyed a dry, rocky landscape. Tuba City had to be somewhere! It was still light, and a few miles away I saw a city. Tuba City! Ahead of me now was a mile-long descent - freshly paved! I got off my bike, kissed the road, and was overjoyed that this day was finally coming to an end. Ruth jumped out of the car, thinking I had gone crazy, and ordered me back on the bike. I wordlessly pointed to Tuba City. In 30 minutes I would be in bed. What a day. Two broken bikes and this never-ending detour!

While I slept, my crew had a lot to do. The sequence of activities was precisely planned so that the next stage could start without delays. There were about two and a half hours during which the bikes were checked, the electronic shifting charged, the lights changed and their batteries charged. Since my team wanted to give me maximum rest during my break and avoid entering my room as much as possible, they allowed us to use all the plugs in the lobby of the hotel. Then the bikes were transferred to the current support vehicle. In the meantime, as quickly as possible, the laundry had to be washed, dried and re-sorted according to the weather conditions. At least for this purpose, it was of immense advantage that the washing and drying cycle of an average American washing machine never takes more than an hour. The first question at the front desk was therefore always immediately where the laundry room was located. The shock was therefore deep when it turned out that the hotel here in Tuba City did not provide any of these machines and the laundromat across the street had already been closed for hours. We were saved that evening in the person of the receptionist's niece, who lived in a apartment protected by barbed wire and guarded by three watchdogs on the other side of the road, with heavy traffic even at this late hour. Despite the advice of the receptionist not to cross the street alone at this late hour, there was no other option if the sharp time table should not be stressed. The laundry changed owner by being thrown over the fence of the well-protected apartment community and under observation of two watchdogs. Not much later it was returned to the team, clean and fresh. How incredibly relieved and grateful we were for this support!

Leadership Lesson 4: Be meticulous in planning, but flexible in execution

For my goal of completing the Race Across America in less than eleven days, I developed a detailed plan, as I mentioned earlier. I analyzed the route, calculated finish times for each Time Station (55 in total), the average speeds required to achieve them, and we booked hotels along the route. To do this, I had to analyze the topography of the course, consider the temperatures and wind conditions on the plains, plan for breaks, and factor in any special events (like delays due to breakdowns). I analyzed the times of other RAAM participants who had completed the course in eleven days, read their blogs, books, and interviews, and derived my plan from them. I developed a plan for my support team and defined their roles. I figured out when I would use which bike, designed a nutrition plan, dealt with all the problems that could arise during the race and searched in race diaries, interviews and video documentations for ideas on how to solve them. This resulted in countless Excel lists with schedules, flowcharts and checklists. I summarized everything in a manual of about 40 pages. The effort was enormous.

On the second day of the race, our plan was already put to the test. The rerouting due to the forest fires near Flagstaff threw our hotel and route planning into disarray. The two defects on the race bikes forced us to take additional breaks and put our schedule in danger. We had to fundamentally reschedule to make the 81-hour grace period in Durango.

If you read the current management literature on planning, you get the impression that planning has gone out of fashion: "No business plan survives the first contact with the customer" and "Nobody except venture capitalists and the late Soviet Union demand 5-year plans," you hear, for example, from Steve Blank, the U.S. entrepreneur and book author. As soon as a long-term plan is released, it becomes already obsolete. How can you make detailed plans if no one can foresee the future? This may all be true, but it neglects a very essential function of planning. This can best be told with a story that can be read at Carl Weick.[49]

> "This incident, narrated by the Hungarian Nobel Prize winner Albert Szent-Gyorgyi and preserved in a poem by Holub (1977), happened during wartime manoeuvres in Switzerland. The young lieutenant of a small Hungarian detachment in the Alps sent a reconnaissance unit into the icy wilderness. It began to snow immediately, snowed for two days and the unit did not return. The lieutenant suffered, fearing that he had dispatched his own people to death. But the third day the unit came back. Where had they been? How had they made their way? Yes, they said, we considered ourselves lost and waited for the end. And then one of us found a map in his pocket. That calmed us down. We pitched camp, lasted out the snowstorm, and then with the map we discovered our bearings. And here we are."[50]

When the lieutenant took a look at the map, he was amazed: It was not a map of the Swiss Alps at all, but a map of the Pyrenees! How can you find the right way with the wrong map? That is, of course, an interesting question. But the much more exciting question is: What would have happened if the soldier had not pulled out the wrong map? Would they have set off together full of confidence? Probably not. Probably they would have lost hope. Perhaps they would have given up. Maybe the group would have broken up and the soldiers would have left in different directions. Perhaps the soldiers would not have been able to mobilize at all or would have fallen out.

Plans are like false maps. Since we are all not clairvoyants, we cannot develop accurate plans. No one can predict the future, but we can shape it. By planning, we make decisions. And through these decisions we shape the future. Sometimes a wrong map does the trick. A plan gives us orientation, mobilizes us, gives us hope and confidence. Planning is a structured examination of a possible future. We set goals, consider alternatives and decide. Should something unforeseen happen, we can govern more easily and quickly. Dwight D. Eisenhower put it in a nutshell: "Plans are useless, but planning is indispensable!", and management guru Peter Drucker writes: "Napoleon allegedly said that no successful battle ever followed his plan. Yet Napoleon planned every one of his battles, far more meticulously than any earlier general had done. Without an action plan, the executive becomes a prisoner of events. And without check-ins to re-examine the plan as events unfold, the executive has no way of knowing which events really matter and which are only noise."[51]

To embark on a project like the Race Across America without planning would be naïve and foolish. To stand at the starting line without having an idea of what might happen, without having thought about how to get through the race, what challenges await you, and to have gone through the race without any if-then scenarios is inconceivable to me. Due to the detour and breakdowns on the second day of the race, the first cut-off in Durango was in jeopardy. If I hadn't been there within 81 hours, the race organizers would have taken me out of the race. In my preparations, I dealt with all the contingencies. One scenario was indeed that the cut-off could be tight - I had planned for relatively long sleep breaks. My third sleep break was planned for Cortez - 70 kilometers before Durango. When it became apparent that it might be tight, we moved the break from Cortez to Durango to a hotel just past Time Station! We had if-then plans, so hardly a glitch upset us!

Psychologist Robert Epstein found in a study of over 3,000 people that planning is an effective way to reduce stress: "Fighting stress before it even starts, planning things rather than making them happen, means planning your day, your year, and your life in a way that minimizes stress."[52] Thinking about obstacles in advance and how to overcome them gives us a sense of control. A sense of control motivates us to take action. Things aren't so scary when we're in control. It's not so much about really having things under control, it's enough if we have the feeling of control. And planning gives us that feeling.[53]

My detailed planning gave me optimism and confidence. Even the incidents on the second day of the race, which completely thwarted our plans, did not throw us off course. My crew found solutions with calm and composure. We constantly compared the actual times with the target times in the plan. The check-ins told us that we had to move the sleep break from Cortez to Durango so that the delays would not jeopardize the 81-hour cut-off time. However, these flexible adjustments did not change our strategy, which we stuck to. As of the fourth day of racing, we were back on schedule.

Day 3 - Monument Valley

At the hotel, everything went pretty routinely: sleeping pill, showers, medical examination and massages. I fell asleep immediately, I didn't even notice the massage. Nor did I notice that Alex and Liane were putting on my compression stockings! When I woke up after three hours, I looked at the clock. I knew the route from Tuba City to Monument Valley. I did some quick math and realized that Monument Valley sunrise was out. What an experience! I thought about what to wear for the photos. I even chose the color of my socks to match the jersey.

It was after midnight when we took off. Tuba City is 1500 meters above sea level, and the night was pleasantly cool. During the first two hours I was constantly fighting against fatigue. Zoli, Florian and Balázs accompanied me and tried to entertain me. I was connected to the follow vehicle via radio. We played Trivial Pursuit, talked about anything, or I listened to music coming from a speaker mounted on the car. It was beginning to dawn, and the outlines of the rock formations were becoming visible. At the entrance to Monument Valley we took a short break and enjoyed the overwhelming beauty of the landscape. At this hour there were no tourists yet. After a few minutes, the media crew caught up and accompanied us through the red-brown landscape. The glowing rocks in the sunrise and the color play of the clouds painted an indescribable picture. This experience alone compensated for everything we had suffered through the previous day.

Unfortunately, nothing came of the easier stage on this race day. I still assumed that I had a somewhat shorter stage ahead of me, I had come much further than planned the day before. But Zoli decided otherwise. Due to the detour and the technical problems - there were also punctures - we had lost a lot of time. The cut-off time in Durango was at stake. We had to arrive there by 9 p.m. at the latest. We cancelled the sleep break in Cortez - about 70 kilometers before Durango. It would have been too close. Instead, the crew booked a hotel in Durango, right after the Time Station. Only there I would be able to sleep again.

Forrest Gump Point. (Photo: Martin Ebster)

After Monument Valley, the media team said goodbye to us and went ahead. They took the two broken bikes to Durango for repair. There was a widely known bike store and repair shop there. The guys explained to the bike store team that we were competing in RAAM and desperately needed their help. The mechanic was less than impressed; the first available repair appointment wasn't for another two weeks! By all means my crew tried to convince them to repair the bikes. But the fact that we were competing in RAAM could not convince them, the Tyrolean charm worked a little better then. Martin Ebster is the tourism director of St. Anton am Arlberg, Roland Volderauer is the managing director of the Stubai Tourism Association, and Hubert Siller is a professor of tourism and leisure management at the Innsbruck Management Center. Surely people in Colorado are familiar with the skiing stronghold of St. Anton am Arlberg? They didn't know St. Anton, but they did know the bike Eldorado of Leogang in Salzburg. When they found a mutual acquaintance in Leogang, the ice was finally broken, and when my crew mentioned our fundraising project and stressed how important it was to finish the race, they had won over the team at the bike store. The guys there repaired my bikes, the work taking most of the day. The news that I would get my Venge and my Tarmac back in the Rocky Mountains gave me wings. Full of motivation, I now continued.

Also on this day it was still quite hot. Before the first climbs towards Durango, which is at about 2000 meters, the RAAMbulance Car with Ruth, Alex and Liane took over my care again. Again and again I overtook other cyclists, and others overtook me. It was an entertaining interplay. Ahead of me now was a very long, relatively easy climb. The landscape was still desert-like, and it was blisteringly hot. My support vehicle drove ahead and waited for me at the top. Alex got out and ran towards me with a bottle of water. In the meantime, Ruth and Liane looked for a suitable place to park - after all, a rule stipulates that a support vehicle must be at least 1.5 meters from of the fog line or the pavement edge of the road. This was not always easy in the mountains and desert. It was not uncommon for support vehicles to get stuck in the sand if they strayed too far onto the shoulder. It is particularly dangerous to stop over dry grass, which can easily catch fire from the heat of the car. That, too, had already happened at RAAM. There is a photo on social media of a crew member smiling at the camera, his burning vehicle in the background. So Alex had gotten out and was now several hundred meters from the support vehicle when she handed me a bottle of water. Jokingly, I asked her if they had forgotten her here. She laughed and said, "Yes." I continued on, and on the hill at the top were Ruth and Liane with the car. We were high-fiving. It must have been close to 7:00. From 7 p.m. on, it's Night Time. Night Time means that the cyclist must move in the headlights of the car during the so-called "direct follow". Under no circumstances may he be found alone in the dark. That would be a disqualification reason. Ruth and Liane realized that there was not enough time left to go back and pick up Alex. They couldn't wait for her to run to them either. They had to be right behind! The two of them started the car, closed in on me, and left Alex standing there - in the middle of Nowhere! They trusted that Alex would somehow know how to help himself. There was a bit of traffic, other teams were on the road, and pretty sure someone would give her a ride. Alex was lucky, Christian Mauduit's support vehicle was behind her. She waved it out, explained the situation, and the French offered to give her a ride. It wasn't quite that comfortable, as the car was already full. Alex was sitting on the lap of a French crew member, but she was saved and soon back with her team!

I reached Durango at dusk - in the rain. And to my surprise, I spotted my media vehicle. Since we had canceled the rooms in Cortez, Hubert, Roland and Martin actually wanted to drive on and should already be far ahead. At short notice, however, they had decided to sleep in Durango after all - but there was no room left. The crew of the American Phil Fox had spent the night in the same hotel in Durango and was just about to leave. When they heard the story, they gave us their room without hesitation. That's the kind of camaraderie between teams that you always see at RAAM. The first cut-off was done. My third sleep break. After that, I was finally off to the Rocky Mountains.

Day 4 - The Rocky Mountains

It was ten degrees Celsius and I could barely feel my fingers. My feet were cold, and I was shivering when I got off the bike in Durango. Completely soaked and exhausted, my crew accompanied me to the hotel room. I was worried about the weather. We were at 2000 meters above sea level, and Wolf Creek Pass at 3300 meters lay ahead. I didn't even want to imagine how I was going to continue toward the pass after two hours of sleep in the rain. The thought of reaching the pass after midnight in snowfall wasn't exactly motivating. Conditions that I still remembered from 2019 - it was snowing then. The descent in such conditions is not only ice cold, but also quite dangerous.

The climbs in the Rocky Mountains are pleasant to ride with seven to eight percent grades and road conditions that are more reminiscent of a highway than a mountain road. There are hardly any switchbacks, so it's easy to reach 80 mph or more on the descents. I asked the girls to keep an eye on the rain radar. If it was still raining after two hours of sleep, but the weather was forecast to improve, they should let me sleep another two or three hours. They nodded and didn't say much about it. The procedures in the hotel were as usual: sleeping pill, brushing teeth, shower, massage. Waking up was already much harder for me than the first nights. I no longer woke up on my own, and it took me a few minutes to come to. I sat up in bed and saw the rain gear the girls had prepared for me. We had agreed, hadn't we, that if it rained we would take a longer break from sleeping? At least that's how I had perceived it, and now they were sending me up Wolf Creek Pass in the middle of the night in sub-ten-degree temperatures and rain! My crew's decision was the right one, of course. We were slightly behind schedule and didn't want to lose any more time. We had only done 1500 kilometers, and the big difficulties were still ahead of us. The target time was eleven days - that was the whole plan. I was also aiming for eleven days so that - should there be any major problems toward the end of the race - I would still have a whole day's leeway to reach the finish within the maximum twelve-day limit.

So off we went. The RAAMerica Car with Bob, Darlene and Bill took the first shift of escort. It was about 9pm and pouring rain. I had a 1300-meter climb ahead of me. This was basically good, because I stayed warm during the climb, and there was an escort car waiting at the top of Wolf Creek Pass where I could warm up and get dry and warm for the long descent.

About half an hour into relatively flat terrain, I began to wonder when it would finally go up to the pass. I had been sure that the climb would start right after the hotel. Around every curve, I expected a steeper pass road, but it never came. Another half hour later - I was already completely soaked - I asked another time. Again I got the same feedback from Bill in the support vehicle, the climb would start in "about 60 miles". 60 miles?!? That couldn't be right. Where was I? In the Rocky Mountains? In the direction of Wolf Creek Pass? I didn't know my way around anymore. Something wasn't right. I rode on, and after a few minutes I asked again and asked him to check the route book. He pretended to do the math and said again, "60 miles." I was horrified. Completely soaked, frozen and barely awake, this news was bad news for me. At least four more hours to the pass! This could not be true. I rode on in the pouring rain, fighting fatigue and looking at the bike computer every few minutes - I was barely moving. My cycling shoes had already soaked up water, and with every pedal stroke I felt it pouring out from between my toes. How nice it would have been if I could have stayed in the warm bed until the rain was over, and then rested and recovered to cross the Rocky Mountains.

Four hours later we reached Pagosa Springs. Here I wanted to take a break, after a few hours with temperatures in the single digits and the rain I was totally down. It was after midnight and I was shivering all over. I'm sure there were gas stations or a

McDonald's in Pagosa Springs, though. A 20-minute break with hot coffee in the warm and dry, that idea kept me fighting. We went past the first houses, and from a distance I saw a gas station on the left side of the road - the only one far and wide. I turned off, rode there, put the bike down and wanted to go in. Closed! That couldn't be true. It was still raining lightly, and there wasn't even an awning. Bill prepared my camping chair, I dropped into it and got something to eat. Now I was sitting in the rain, in the middle of the Rocky Mountains, in the middle of the night. A nightmare. I was a mess. After a few minutes I asked when the next crew change was scheduled.

"In about 20 minutes!" was the answer.

It didn't make any sense now to get back on the bike and take the next break in 20 minutes. I guess it was all a big misunderstanding. If I had known that in such a short time there would be the next crew change, which we always combined with a short break for me, I would have went on for these few more minutes. My support crew, however, had been watching me suffer for hours, so they simply gave in to my request for a break. They must have felt incredibly sorry for me. They could see the state I was in. I sat down in the car, we turned the heating to the highest level and waited until the RAAMbler Car with Zoli, Florian and Balázs arrived.

We must have been standing in Pagosa Springs for almost an hour before we moved on. It was still raining. After only a mile, I saw a few open gas stations and a couple of fast food restaurants. We only had to drive five minutes further and I would have had everything I dreamed of.

I can hardly remember the next 30 kilometers to the climb, but somehow I had found my way back into my rhythm. It was drizzling only lightly and heavy fog enveloped us. The climb of seven to eight percent was not a big strain, I felt strong and climbed slowly but steadily up the 1200 meters of altitude. It was completely silent - kind of spooky. At some point I saw a light in the fog. It could not be a car. Nor could it be the top of the pass. It was about 2 o'clock in the morning, and I had been on the road again for a while. I approached the light and suddenly saw a figure coming towards me. Hubert! The media team was there! It appeared somewhere at any time of day or night, always a highlight for me. In the middle of the loneliness suddenly a few familiar faces. Hubert walked a few meters beside me, we exchanged a few words, Martin was behind the camera and cheered me on, and Roland, as always, had some good jokes.

Around 5 o'clock I reached Wolf Creek Pass - it is the highest point of the race, Continental Divide, at 3309 meters. I stopped, we took photos and did a short interview for K19. I changed my clothes and put on pretty much everything I had for the long descent. Even my down ski touring jacket, which I had packed only for extreme weather conditions. I felt really warm for the first time in hours, started the descent and was chilled out after a few minutes. To keep warm, I tried to pedal along at a speed of 60 to 70 km/h. But that didn't have any effect. At the end of the descent I was completely frozen and needed another short warm-up break.

Now a long plateau lay ahead of me: at over 2300 meters above sea level, it was flat for about 100 kilometers until the ascent to La Veta Pass, the third highest point of the race at 2900 meters.

Here in the area, near Alamosa, being in the leading position, Rainer Steinberger had crashed heavily after 1800 kilometers. Due to a bump on the shoulder, Rainer crashed and was seriously injured: His left collarbone and two ribs were broken. He spent some time in hospital before being transferred back to Bavaria. The lead was then taken by Nicole Reist from Switzerland. She was in the lead for days before a dramatic turnaround. So it said on the media release on their homepage:

"Since the German Rainer Steinberger had to give up the race after three days due to an injury caused by a crash, the Swiss rider was constantly far ahead, usually with a lead of more than 100 kilometers over the fastest man. She had already completed 2800 of the 3037 miles, was in the middle of the Appalachians, her favorite mountains, and was on the way to the big sensation - then it happened: During an evasive maneuver she crashed and had extremely severe pain in her thigh afterwards. It took around four hours before she was checked out by the team doctor and found fit enough to continue. This break was too long even for her big lead. Just at the end of the standstill, Australian Allan Jefferson overtook her. A head-to-head race began, Nicole Reist was able to overtake her competitor again after a short time and keep him at a distance for hours. Another crash from a standing start -

Reist was unable to click out of the pedal quickly enough due to her thigh ailment - as well as persistent pain then decided the race after around 2950 miles: The Swiss could no longer maintain her pace and had to let the Australian go. Then the complete collapse, so that she was even overtaken by the Czech Svata Bozak a few miles before the finish."

Nicole Reist then won the women's classification despite her adductor problems and a broken rib, but she was bitterly disappointed. She wrote to me on Facebook after the race that she would have liked to wait for me at the finish line, but she was no longer able to do so due to her injuries.

So now I was on this plateau in the Rocky Mountains, and once again I got cramp-like stomach pains. The issue of digestion is a major challenge for all Race Across America participants, as it takes up to about 15,000 calories to meet the body's daily energy needs during this extreme continuous effort. 15,000 calories is roughly equivalent to 30 plates of Spaghetti Bolognese, 15 Wiener Schnitzels with fries or 30 Big Macs. The intake of these amounts of solid food alone is almost inconceivable. Anyone who has ever enjoyed a Big Mac meal and then sat in an aero position on a racing bike knows that it is impossible to perform when so stuffed. So because no ultra-endurance athlete, no matter how trained, can digest such quantities, most athletes resort to a more or less exclusive diet of liquid food. Thus, the body does not lose "unnecessary" energy through digestive work. Nevertheless, the restricted blood flow during endurance exercise and additional problems such as shock and heat stress ensure a very slow gastrointestinal passage and therefore cause discomfort for many athletes.

Apart from the pure number of calories, one should, especially as an athlete, pay attention to a balanced distribution of macronutrients (such as carbohydrates, fats and protein) and ensure the supply of minerals and vitamins to the body. In the short term, you might be able to cover your energy needs with "calorie bombs", sweets and cola, but even if you were spared digestive problems, a drop in performance sooner or later would be almost certain.

Accordingly, nutrition is one of the biggest problems and can become a huge mental burden. If the calorie intake doesn't work, you have to reckon with enormous weight loss, if you make it to the finish line at all.

For all these reasons, I decided to use high-calorie liquid food. My sponsor Fresubin provided me with the appropriate products. With liquid food, you can consume this enormous number of calories easily and quickly and ensure an adequate supply of nutrients to the body. Per 200-milliliter bottle, I thus took in about 400 calories; there are drinks in all kinds of flavors. My goal was to consume about 500 calories per hour. For this, there was a detailed nutrition protocol, which was pedantically kept by my crew. My weight was noted every day, as was every single toilet break.

From my experiences at the Race Around Austria, I knew that my body first had to adjust to liquid food. I had learned that I got digestive problems after three to four days, but they improved again after another one or two days. Therefore, I switched to liquid food already four days before the start. I ate about 95 percent liquid food for two whole weeks. In between I got a banana, a sandwich, a muffin or a similar small reward every now and then. In Indiana, I even got to eat a slice of pizza!

Nutritional protocol.

Despite this acclimatization phase, I already had slight gastrointestinal problems before the Rocky Mountains. For "emergencies" of this kind - should there be no gas station or no restaurant nearby - we had a bucket, garbage bags and a poncho with us. We did not want to receive a time penalty for an outdoor toilet break. "Public nudity, urination, defecation, lewd or indecent behavior" are, after all, forbidden by the rulebook. My toilet tactics actually worked quite well, with a few exceptions. In the desert, however, the sand was so hot that the plastic bucket became soft and the toilet break was probably anything but restful for my thighs.

So, on the high plateau in the Rocky Mountains, my digestion was now becoming a problem. In the meantime, the RAAMbulance car with the three ladies had taken over, and we were on a busy highway. Along the sides of the road there was nothing but flat grass for miles - not a shrub, not a bush, not a tree behind which I could have disappeared with my bucket. So I wanted to know from my crew how far I had to go to get to the next town. The answer was, "16 miles!" A whole hour! Somehow it had to work out. The support vehicle was already pulling ahead to prepare my bathroom stop, we always did that. A gas station or fast food restaurant was sought, the crew asked permission for me to use the restroom, and combined the stop with a gas stop or shopping. My girls had located Lu's Mainstreet Cafe just down the road in Alamosa. As I approached it, I saw Ruth, Alex and Liane waving at me from a distance.

"All set!" said Ruth, escorting me into the crowded restaurant - it was around lunchtime.

Thunderous applause broke out when I entered the pub. Ruth, in her euphoria, had let the whole place know that a Race Across America rider was now coming to make a bathroom stop here. In this small town, that was a sensation. There was probably not much other variety for the inhabitants there. Only an older man with a long, gray beard didn't seem to be so enthusiastic. When I left the restaurant after a few minutes, I noticed that the man was literally rushing to the toilet. During the next break, the girls - who could hardly contain their laughter - told me the back story. Ruth had run into the pub and announced loudly that a RAAM rider would be coming in a few minutes and needed the toilet. The pub owners and patrons found this very amusing and waited for me. Ruth went back to the car to get something, but then went right back to guard the restroom. Once inside the pub, she noticed that the restroom door was locked. Someone was inside. She yanked open the unlocked door and saw an older man with a long, gray beard sitting on the toilet. She asked him what he was doing, after all, the toilet was reserved for me. He said it was urgent, he was having digestive problems. Ruth had a good answer ready: She was a pharmacist and he got everything he needed for his stomach, but he had to get out of there right now. The man - visibly surprised - pulled up his pants, left the toilet without a word and left the restroom to me.

From Alamosa it was a very pleasant climb to La Veta Pass (2873 m) and then a rapid descent to the next sleep break. As the valley opened up in front of me, I could see towards Cucharas Pass (3092 m), the third and last pass of the Rocky Mountains. The view, however, was not very uplifting: a huge black wall of clouds that blocked the mountain like a steel curtain! Oh no! It was afternoon, I had made up some time, I had a two-hour sleep break ahead of me, and I was supposed to tackle the last 3000m at around 7pm. Not again in heavy rain and freezing cold!!!

Leadership Lesson 5: Know your why

As I sat in my camping chair in the middle of the night in the Rocky Mountains, completely soaked and frozen through, during a short break at the closed gas station in the rain, disappointed that I couldn't get any hot coffee and couldn't warm up anywhere, I began to ask myself why I was doing all this to myself. I had 1500 kilometers behind me. The 51-degree heat in the desert had taken a toll on me, the problems with the detour on the second day and the two broken bikes were taking a toll on me mentally, and now the rain, cold, and sleep deprivation were really getting to me. Why am I doing all this to myself? I haven't even finished a third of the race and I'm already reaching my physical and mental limits! I was now feeling the full brutality of the Race Across America and knew that this was all just the beginning. While these thoughts were running through my mind, I watched Bob discussing the race with Bill and looked into their distraught faces. At that moment, I remembered something Bob had told me after our 2017 four-team RAAM and also mentioned in his talks. We had been on the road for six days at that point, Bob was exhausted, and last night had taken everything out of him: "As I was racing in RAAM 2017 on Saturday morning June 24th at 3am in the very cold, hard, driving, miserable rain, I could have easily quit ... and then the thought came to mind that kids who contract polio don't get to quit ... they are in for LIFE!!!" Bob would have loved to quit under these harsh conditions, but the thought of children with polio stopped him. Bob decided to keep going, he didn't give up. We finished, and that year we raised over $500,000 in donations to eradicate polio.

We were not racing just for us, we had a mission! I was now thinking about this mission. I had to get to the finish line. With each Time Station I made, more donations came in. I had posted a RAAM End Polio Challenge weeks before the start. Numerous Rotary Clubs sponsored a Time Station and donated to our project when I passed it. I was aware that RAAM would be difficult, and I knew I would be pushed to my limits. But I wasn't doing it just for me: "We ride so that others can walk!" That was our motto, that was our why. What I was going through is nothing compared to what children go through when they get polio. Those thoughts got me back on the bike.

Viktor Frankl, founder of logotherapy and existential analysis, survived four concentration camps in Nazi Germany: Theresienstadt, Auschwitz, Kaufering and Türkheim, where he was finally liberated by the US Army. His experiences and impressions in the concentration camps he described in numerous publications. His book "Man's Search for Meaning"[54] sold over ten million copies. In this book he explores the question of what determines the will to survive. Viktor Frankl was convinced that we always - under all circumstances - have the freedom to decide:

"Even though conditions such as lack of sleep, insufficient food and various mental stresses may suggest that the inmates were bound to react in certain ways, in the final analysis it becomes clear that the sort of person the prisoner became was the result of an inner decision, and not the result of camp influences alone. Fundamentally, therefore, any man can, even under such circumstances, decide what shall become of him-mentally and spiritually."[55]

Viktor Frankl observed that those inmates of concentration camps who had a why were significantly more likely to leave the camp alive than those who had lost all hope. Frankl further observed that those prisoners who survived, who had found a way to persevere, had always had a larger goal that carried them through the most difficult conditions. For some, it was a child who had found refuge in a distant land and would be waiting for them after liberation. For others, it was a spouse or family member. For still others, it was an unfinished task or a creative work that required their unique contribution.[56] In his book, Frankl writes, " The prisoner who had lost faith in the future – his future – was doomed. With his loss of belief in the future he also lost his spiritual hold; he let himself decline and become subject to mental and physical decay."[57] When he worked in the camp's hospital in 1944, he noticed that the death rate had increased particularly dramatically between Christmas and New Year's Day. Many camp inmates had had naive hopes of being liberated before Christmas. As the end of the year approached, they realized that nothing had changed in their situation; they lost courage and hope. This affected their resilience and their ability to survive. Viktor Frankl recorded in the words of Nietzsche, " He who has a why to live for can bear almost any how.!"

I kept keeping in mind our why: "We ride so that others can walk!" This why, this greater purpose, was an important motivation for me. Whenever things got tough, I made myself aware of what the higher purpose was. This why always gave me the strength to endure the pain and persevere.

Exercise scientist Tim Noakes conducted a fascinating experiment in strength training in the 1990s.[58] He had athletes lift weights until muscle failure. When they dropped the weights and could no longer lift weights because the muscles no longer contracted, he applied electrical sensors, stimulated the muscles and was able to show that they were still able to contract. Although the athletes could no longer contract their muscles voluntarily, they still had reserves. Physical exhaustion - Noakes concluded - initially occurs psychologically, not physically. Although there are still physical reserves, our brain plays the role of a regulator and pulls the plug to protect us from injury and organ failure. In their compelling book, "Peak Performance,"[59] Brad Stulberg and Steve Magness cite numerous athletes who were able to mobilize the last few percent of their reserves and perform at peak levels because they were driven by a higher purpose. They write:

"When we focus on a self-transcending purpose that goes beyond ourself and our life, we are capable of far more than we thought possible. Victor Strecher, a professor of public health, argues that this because when we focus intensely on something larger than ourselves. Thereby our ego is minimized. As it is our ego fulfils the role of protecting us or our self it leads us to escape when we are threatened. We can however overcome the fears, our worries, and our physiological protective mechanisms, when transcend our self and stop paying attention to our ego. So we can overcome the protective mechanisms that often hold us back. By focusing on a self-transcending purpose we can achieve major breakthroughs and a vast spectrum of possibilities opens up."[60]

Athletes who compete in a race not for themselves but for others, for example for their children, for the family or for the team, can mobilize more reserves than those who compete only for themselves.

John Coleman, author of the book "Crafting Your Purpose,"[61] speaks of a crisis of purpose that many people are facing. A Gallup study of more than 2,000 college graduates found that more than 50 percent cannot find a meaningful job. However, the well-being of those graduates who have meaningful work is nearly ten times higher.[62] Fewer than 20 percent of executives report feeling a strong, deeper sense of inner purpose.[63] At the same time, many studies show how important a "sense of purpose" is. People who see a deeper purpose for their lives are less likely to suffer from depression, anxiety, boredom and loneliness. They have a lower probability of developing Alzheimer's disease, have better chances of surviving cancer, have higher life satisfaction and a 15 percent lower risk of dying an early death.[64] So it pays to think about the deeper meaning of one's life or work. Every job and activity has elements of purpose and fun in it, and in everything we do, we should balance purpose and fun. [65]

To do this, do a short exercise as suggested by John Coleman in his book.[66] We can classify all activities in our job or in our life according to how meaningful we consider them to be (meaningful and without meaning) and how much pleasure and fun we get out of them (with fun and pleasure, without fun and pleasure). Now distribute everything you do on a typical day or in a typical week to four quadrants of a 2x2 matrix:

- Drudgery (meaningful and important, but without fun and joy): These are all those activities that are important and must be done. However, they are no fun and are pure fulfillment of duty.
- Superficialities: Tasks that are fun but have no particular meaning.
- Misery: Work that is neither fun nor has any deeper meaning.
- Fulfillment: Activities that fill us with fun and joy and that are important and meaningful.

	Without fun and joy	With fun and joy
Meaningful	**Drudgery:** These are all those activities that are important and must be done. However, they are no fun and are pure fulfillment of duty.	**Fulfillment:** Activities that fill us with fun and joy and that are important and meaningful.
Without meaning	**Misery:** Work that is neither fun nor has any deeper meaning.	**Superficialities:** Tasks that are fun but have no particular meaning.

How meaningful is your life?[67]

How is your time distributed among the individual quadrants? Where do most of your tasks and activities fall? What can you change about them? How can you set new priorities? How can you find more meaning in your tasks? It is worthwhile to think about these questions.

If much of your time falls under the categories of "drudgery" or "misery," you should think about what the deeper meaning might be and how you can derive more joy from these tasks. It's often just up to us to find the meaning or enjoyment in such jobs. Curtis Jenkins, for example, is a school bus driver. It's a tough and often boring job. A CBS report covered how Jenkins turned his undoubtedly responsible but boring job into a lot of fun for himself and for the kids. He created a "Yellow Bus Utopia": all the kids on the bus were assigned roles of some sort, such as police officer, secretary, CEO, administrative assistant, etc. In this way, he wanted to create a community where children took responsibility. The bus ride became an important community experience for the children and a meaningful educational task for Curtins Jenkins that was fun and fulfilling[68].

Many of our daily tasks have an impact on other people, and it's when we become aware of what we can positively impact that we can often first see the meaning. Adam Grant, a professor at the Wharton School, describes in a study how fundraisers at a call center realized the importance of their work when they were introduced to the students who benefited from the money they raised through their activities. Fundraisers who personally knew the beneficiaries of their work spent 142 percent more time on the phone with potential donors and raised 171 percent more funds than fundraisers who did not know the recipients of the donations.[69] So think about what meaning your work has for others; from this, it's often easy to derive a deeper meaning for your own activity.

Another technique to identify meaning in one's work is the "task hierarchy" (Action Identification Theory).[70] Viewed at the lowest level, I'm just typing letters at the moment. Considered at a higher level, I'm writing a book. And at the highest level, I may be helping people become more productive, more successful, and more satisfied. You may know the anecdote of the three stonemasons attributed to Michelangelo:[71]

A man arrives at a construction site where three stonemasons are working diligently. Externally, there is no difference. He goes to the first one and asks: What are you doing there? The latter looks at him puzzled and says: "I earn my living here. The man goes on and comes to the second stonemason. He asks him the same question. The latter looks at him with shining eyes, visibly proud, and says: I am the best stonemason in the whole country. Again, the man goes on and comes to the third. He asks him the same question. He thinks for a moment and then says: I am helping to build a cathedral here.

Apply this idea of task hierarchy to your work! What is the overriding sense?

Finally, think about how much time you spend pointlessly, for example with your smartphone! You can check your screen time via app on a daily basis and track how much time you spend with individual apps. This is often hours, with much of this time falling under "superficialities." Consciously reduce these times, introduce a "screen-free time", like US actress Jennifer Aniston, for example. Use these times for activities that fulfill you. When looking for such tasks, ask yourself the following questions: What am I particularly good at? What activities fulfill me so much that I forget about time and everything around me becomes a minor matter? What achievements am I particularly proud of? What gives me a sense of achievement and the feeling that I am developing? What contribution do I make to others and from which relationships do I draw energy?[72]

Let us come back to Viktor Frankl. Those inmates of the concentration camps who still saw a meaning or still had a purpose were more likely to survive. Those who had a why imagined the outcome as they went through all the suffering and hardships. They thought about what it would be like when they saw their family or children again. That imagination kept them going. This leads us to the next lesson: visualize the goal!

Leadership Lesson 6: Visualize your goal

There is one mental technique that is used by the world's best athletes virtually without exception: Visualization.[73] It is one of the most important tools for performance improvement and motivation.[74] Vivid visualization of the result of all efforts is an important motivational support during training and during the race, especially when the going gets tough. Christoph Strasser, the six-time Race Across America winner and 24-hour world record holder, said in an interview:

> "A good exercise - whether on an indoor bike or on the couch - is to close your eyes for ten minutes and visualize the moment when you cross the finish line - how it will feel, what the coaches will say, how it will smell there,

what you will treat yourself to there, what the moment of arrival will look like. If these moments are experienced again and again in the in your mind and one stores the beauty of this this moment, then one can fall back on it, when it does not go so well. Then the subconscious will tell you how great it will be at the finish line, exactly as you imagined it, and the motivation to continue will be there. A very simple exercise, with which you can help yourself a lot and do good. The best thing to do is just close your eyes for ten minutes on the indoor bike and imagine the whole thing - and ten minutes with your eyes closed is a long time!"[75]

I used this technique for myself. I painted pictures in my head and tried to imagine what it will be like when I reach my big goal. What it will be like to cross the finish line in Annapolis after 5,000 kilometers of endless exertion and symbolically hand over the donation check. I visualized all the great challenges: How I survived the heat in the desert, the moment I passed Wolf Creek Pass, how I crossed the Mississippi Bridge and tackled the last hills in the Appalachian Mountains. I imagined my crew with me, enjoying those moments, and those feelings carrying us to Annapolis. Every time I went on a training ride, I thought about it. Those images burned into my brain. Whenever things got tough, during training or during the race, when my motivation waned or I was in pain, I would recall those images and they would displace my negative feelings. For my visualization exercises, I followed the recommendations of mental coach Patrick Cohn:

1. "Visualize the outcome you want – When you mentally rehearse your performance in your head, make sure you see the event as how you want it to unfold. If your mental images turn negative, stop the mental tape, rewind and restart, then visualize again, see the performance you want to see.
2. Use all your senses from a first-person perspective – Visualize your sports performance in detail. What would you see, hear, feel, smell and taste. Feel how your body would feel as you go through the motions of your performance. Try adding in some physical movements that coincide with the visualized images. Feel the excitement of successfully fulfilling your performance goal.
3. Practice frequently – Mental rehearsal for athletes is a skill that becomes better with repetition. Practice your visualization or imagery daily.
4. If you want to take advantage of the power of visualization, consult with a Mental Game Coach about incorporating this essential skill into your training."[76]

But during my two participations in the Race Around Austria, the 2200-kilometer nonstop race around Austria, I made another important experience. Visualizing the big goal and finishing successfully is an important exercise, but it's not enough. I discovered how important small intermediate goals - small wins - are. If you don't keep having small feelings of success and progress, sooner or later you will lose your motivation. I already mentioned this before, but it just seems very important to me: When I wanted to give up at the Race Around Austria after about 1500 kilometers with severe knee pain and acute sleep deprivation, in the middle of the night and in the rain, my crew chief Zoli helped me to an important realization. He tried to persuade me to keep going: "Only 30 more kilometers to Innsbruck for the next sleep break, you have to make it!"

I doubted: "Maybe I'll manage that. But after that comes the Kühtai, the Biehlerhöhe and the mountains in Vorarlberg. I'll never make it with this pain!"

Zoli found the right answer: "Forget everything that comes later. Now there is one goal, and that is Innsbruck. There you have a two-hour sleep break. After that, we'll see."

Zoli convinced me, somehow I still made it to Innsbruck. From my sleep break I woke up after two hours by myself. The Kühtai and the remaining mountains we managed with aplomb. The lesson: never think about how far it is, but set yourself small intermediate goals.

My lesson learned:

1. Visualize your big goal. Always think about what it will be like when you reach it - that's where you get your motivation!
2. But never think about how far it is - that leads to frustration!
3. Define small intermediate goals - Small Wins: The next Time Station, the next city, the next sleep break - these feelings of success give you the strength to continue!

I divided the 5,000 kilometers of the Race Across America into eleven daily stages. I pushed aside thoughts like "3458 kilometers to go" or "1864 kilometers to go". Instead, I concentrated on the daily goals and the small intermediate stages. At the end of each daily stage, I rewarded myself with a two- to three-hour sleep break. I divided each daily stage into eight- to nine-hour units - the shift changes of my crew, which meant a 15-minute break for me. I divided each nine-hour unit into three-hour units, after each of which I got a five-minute break. And I divided each three-hour unit further: every 45 minutes I got a bottle of liquid nutrition. In this way, I achieved my small and larger intermediate goals. Each of these intermediate goals meant progress for me and brought me closer to my big goal. The harder it got during the race, the more important they became for me. My crew recognized that, and starting on the seventh or eighth day, I always got my bottle of liquid nutrition with the comment, "Fresubin Time!" A symbolic act that said to me: 45 minutes done again on the way to the big finish in Annapolis!

We often put too much emphasis on the big goal and neglect the importance of small progress. A big goal without small wins quickly loses its appeal. We need a permanent sense that we are making progress. Teresa Amabile, a professor at Harvard Business School, published a highly interesting study on the importance of small wins. Amabile had employees keep daily records of what they experienced - for four months. She evaluated 12,000 diary entries to determine what most contributed to employees experiencing a day as good. Of all the things that positively influence emotions, motivation and perceptions during a workday, progress in meaningful work is the most important.[77] Even the smallest feelings of accomplishment can make a difference. The researcher recognized: The key to performance motivation is to provide a sense of achievement! Therefore, keep a diary - at least a mental one - of your progress. This will be the key to your motivation and stamina.

During my preparations for the Race Across America, I used a second mental technique: reframing! I tried to transform the big difficulties into positive challenges. I mentally prepared myself for all the big dangers: for the heat, for the cold, for wind and rain, for sleep deprivation and pain. By mentally imagining them, these difficulties did not diminish, but they lost their terror. Since I was prepared for them, they were easier to bear. At no moment during the race did it become as hard as I had imagined! If one expresses fears or writes them down, this effect is particularly great.

This is what Sebastian Purps-Pardigol writes in his book "Leben mit Hirn":

> "Fact labeling, however ... is a way of accepting unpleasantness. You describe what is, without trying to change it, and miraculously that already leads to relief, and it's even neurally measurable. Gerardo Ramirez is a professor of developmental psychology at Ball State University, Muncie, Indiana. He researched fact labeling in writing. It's a way to reduce anxiety and increase mental performance. For his research, he recruited students who were near panic-stricken before every math exam. Their excitement was so great that they made an above-average number of errors on these tests. Ramirez had a portion of these pitiful young people write down their worries and fears they had about the upcoming exam for seven minutes immediately before the next exam. So they put all their feelings into words in writing. The result: the error rate of the participants who had carried out this form of fact labeling was significantly reduced in the math test that followed. The subjects made a full 45 percent fewer errors than the control group, which continued to be agitated."[78]

I used a little trick to make my fears even more bearable: I tried to turn the biggest difficulties into positive challenges. Trying to redefine problems as something positive can be very helpful. There's interesting research on this, too. For example, it was found that students who saw test anxiety as something positive did better on tests![79] This reframing of great difficulties into positive challenges worked so well for me that I actually looked forward to the desert, to the Rocky Mountains, to the wind in Kansas. I looked at these challenges as great tests that I had to pass and that were part of the race. I looked forward to the 50 degrees in the desert because I knew if that was behind me, I had overcome a great difficulty and I was closer to my goal.

Day 5 - The Great P(l)ains

I made it to the hotel in La Veta, Colorado, just before the first drops of rain and was asleep within minutes. When I woke up about three hours later, I saw the sun shining in the sky. The thunderstorm had been violent and brief. Zoli let me know that it seemed that the apocalypse was nearing. The RAAMerica Car with Bob, Darlene and Bill now accompanied me up the last pass of the Rocky Mountains. The climb began a few hundred yards behind the hotel. A beautiful landscape with bizarre rock formations marked the way. Somehow, however, I could not really realize what was happening around me. As if in a trance, I climbed meter by meter up the ascent. I reached the pass before nightfall. It was cool, and I changed clothes. At the same time as me, another RAAM participant had reached the top. He did not stop at all and started the descent without getting dressed warmly - incomprehensible for me.

After Cucharas Pass, it was downhill for a bit, then some short climbs before a long descent towards Kansas awaited me.

Finally! Montezuma near Dodge City was my next destination: 529 kilometers, 1960 meters of climbing. With an average of 24 km/h, I wanted to be at the hotel by 5 p.m. - two hours behind my original schedule. Soon it got dark, the descent required a lot of concentration. The road was in a pitiful condition, there were always centimeter-wide longitudinal cracks in the asphalt, five, six centimeters deep. I was also worried about the cattle guards whose crossbars have much larger gaps than in Austria. The best thing was to ride over them at high speed, so you felt the least of the vibration. Some of these cattle guards were not properly sunk into the ground at all and stuck out dangerously high. The greatest danger, however, came from the crossbars, which were not continuous; there was a longitudinal gap in the middle that was several centimeters wide! If you poked in here with the front wheel, a crash could not be avoided.

After an accident-free descent, I was looking forward to the last climb, but I had remembered from previous years the very long and very flat descent following it. Tens of kilometers you could easily ride here at a speed of 50 km / h. I was sure to make up some time again. It came - as almost always - quite differently.

In the meantime, the RAAMbler Car with Zoli, Florian and Balázs had taken over. They drove behind me and illuminated the road for me. From Race Headquarters now came a tornado warning for Colorado, exactly for the section of the track I was on. Soon a heavy crosswind set in, which swept me again and again from the right side of the road to the left. Thank goodness there was no oncoming traffic in this godforsaken area that night. My crew chief pointed to the night sky. To my left, starry night; to my right, not a single star was visible – the tornado! Zoli cheered me on, if I was fast enough I might just escape the twister and the heavy rain. He was right, we only got to feel the remnants of the tornado. Instead of the expected 50 km/h, however, I only managed a speed of 15 and 20 km/h. Nevertheless, I had to fight against the crosswind all the time. Just keeping the bike stable was difficult enough.

Just before the tornado in Colorado. (Photo: Florian Phleps)

The wind got weaker slowly, but continued to blow continuously from the right side. Poor road conditions with expansion joints in the asphalt made riding on the aerobars almost impossible. Every ten or 20 meters I got a heavy blow, and that for dozens of kilometers.

At some point - the sun had long risen - I had to stop. I was extremely tired and was afraid of falling asleep on the bike. I lay down on the passenger seat of the support vehicle for 15 minutes, Florian covered the windshield with a sweatshirt so that the sun didn't shine in my face. A power nap of 15 minutes works wonders in such a phase. Although the body does not recover, alertness, reaction time and cognitive performance can be significantly increased by the short regeneration time. A NASA study of pilots, for example, found that they were 54 percent more alert and performed 34 percent better after a power nap.[80] So sleep deprivation was slowly but surely becoming a bigger problem. I had now been on the road for just under 2,000 kilometers and for about four days, a total of about nine hours of which I had slept.

Colorado - the Rocky Mountains are behind us. (Photo: Hubert Siller)

We passed through Kim, a tiny town in Colorado. After about 100 kilometers the first little town. There was not much to see. Just 74 people live there. In 2019, one of our support vehicles reached the town with an almost empty tank and was happy to find a small self-service gas station. However, all attempts to pay by credit card failed. A truck driver who was refueling her truck observed this and kindly asked if she could help. Andi asked her for her credit card, we could give her cash for a tank of gas. As if it were a matter of course, she helped out. When she learned that we were participating in RAAM and raising funds for polio eradication, she refused to take our money. She paid, thanked us for getting involved in a charity project, and drove on.

We had successfully conquered the desert and the Rocky Mountains. Now began a section of the route that most people are afraid of: Kansas and Missouri, about 1000 kilometers of flat straights with unfavorable wind conditions. Now the battle in the head finally began, and here it became more and more apparent who had the mental strength to finish this race.

For this stage, I had to do without my media team for the most part. Roland had to go back to Austria for work reasons, so Hubert and Martin took him to Wichita in Kansas. From there he flew to Munich. Too bad, I would miss his humor and good mood!

I don't have much to report about Kansas: It was hot, boring, and it stank immensely of decaying animals on the side of the road. Roadkill, as the Americans say. Unbearable! The smell of the cattle ranches, especially near Dodge City, where tens of thousands of animals wait in the heat and on dust-dry ground for their redemption in the slaughterhouse, was appalling. This year it was especially hot and it barely cooled down at night. From the news we learned that about 2000 animals died in the sweltering heat. The roads lead straight for hours without curves. Almost a highlight when the road changes direction after 200 kilometers at a 90-degree angle! You pedal and pedal and have the feeling that you're not making any progress, the landscape just doesn't change.

In 2016, when we were a four-man team here, I made two entries about Kansas in my race diary:

> "There's not much to report for the next thousand kilometers. Flat and monotonous. The grain elevators are the only change in the landscape. Every 10 to 20 kilometers there is one. Sometimes on the left and sometimes on the right. Some are white, others rather gray. I have also seen yellow ones. Sometimes there are three, or four. But often there are five. If you love grain elevators, you'll like it here. There are also combines. Most are very large and made by John Deere. They probably sell a lot of them here. You rarely see small combines... After 140 kilometers straight ahead suddenly a change: a stop sign. Now don't make a mistake. Stop, put your foot on the ground and then continue. There could be a race official standing somewhere watching. We don't want a time penalty. But probably the officials don't like to be it Kansas anyway ...

Kansas is a flat country. Everything is flat here. The roads, the meadows and the fields. Even the animals are flat. The armadillos, for example. Or the raccoons and the rabbits and the snakes. Even turtles are flat here. And dead they are, too. That's probably because of all the trucks. They're not so flat here. Somewhere else where it's not so flat, I like it better. In Tyrol, for example."

As expected, I had to fight with constant crosswind. Florian and Martin kept a record in the Radsportnews race diary:

"The wind from the south continued throughout the stage and was so strong that the support vehicles could barely get the passenger door open. For Kurt, the wind always came from the right and made riding very hard here. A few short connecting roads to the north brought a tailwind. A crew shift right at the Kansas border went perfectly well and we didn't have any technical issues. Around 6:00 p.m. Kurt reached the point where he could finish the stage and take his rest in Dodge City. Tired, annoyed by the constant wind, but mentally and physically still strong, he presented himself upon arrival. The race continues from 10:00 p.m. on, straight ahead for another day with crosswinds or headwinds through Kansas. About 60 kilometers after the start, the halfway line awaits him."

Day 6 - Unbearable pain

Finally, the halfway point! The halfway point was done, that was the good news! But the thought that it would take so long again to reach the finish in Annapolis was unbearable. The first half of the race had been relatively smooth despite all the difficulties. We survived the desert well, the Rocky Mountains and even the strong winds in Kansas could not harm us much. But I was increasingly exhausted and worn out, pain, sleep deprivation and lack of motivation started to become more and more of a problem. In Oceanside, at the start, I had been fresh and fully motivated. But the Halfway Point was a big milestone, I had never cycled that far before. And the same distance was now to come my way again!

> "Started just past Montezuma at 10 p.m. (OZ), Kurt sets off on the second part of the journey across Kansas. The crosswind has meanwhile become a strong headwind. Kurt's succinct comment: 'Headwind is the best training partner.' He makes very good progress during the night and reaches 'Halfway Point', 7.8 miles past the Time Station in Greensburg, around two in the morning. Three of the four support teams are there for this big moment, congratulating Kurt on 2500 kilometers completed. Such actions and videos from fellow athletes give him great motivation. Kurt really enjoys the few minutes with his crew."

For one or two days I was plagued by terrible knee pain, which always started in the breaks. I knew that problem from the Race Around Austria. During my short breaks, the pain was so severe that it made me doubled over in my camping chair. I knew now that this pain would accompany me for the remaining 2500 kilometers. Every three hours, during my short breaks, this ordeal awaited me. I knew that knee pain was normal and that the cause of the pain was not long-term damage. It was merely pain. And so I was able to endure it. During my sleep breaks, I tried to avoid this agony as much as possible by taking sleeping pills and painkillers. Nevertheless, I kept waking up and moaning in pain. Not a pretty outlook for the rest of the race. I realized that now I would have to cope not only with cumulative lack of sleep and exhaustion until the finish, but from now on also with this pain. The only thing that did me some good was massages. Zoli, Ruth, Alex and Liane knew exactly where to squeeze with all their might to relax the muscles. The positive thing was that I knew the pain would improve after a few minutes on the bike. Actually, motivation enough to keep my breaks very short. During the sleep break, Alex, my team doctor, always stayed with me. She massaged me to sleep and once said, "Every time I stop massaging you, you wake up!"

Alex slept about as little as I did and also began to suffer from sleep deprivation. Once it even happened that she fell asleep on me during the sleep break and still while she was massaging me - I hadn't noticed anything.

One day I was in so much pain that Alex had already given me a pain pill during the day, and then I got another one for the sleep break. But when I woke up after about an hour because of the pain, I asked for another one. She agreed, and I instantly fell back asleep. After the race, I learned that the third tablet had been a placebo! Alex could not give me any more, the dose was already high enough, and she knew what role the mind plays in terms of pain.

For the last day or two, my neck was also making itself felt. I was afraid that Shermer's Neck was developing. Shermer's Neck describes a typical Race Across America phenomenon that is one of the most common reasons for a DNF. Due to overuse of the neck muscles, cyclists may be unable to keep their heads upright. Not only is this dangerous because forward vision is restricted, but Shermer's Neck can potentially lead to secondary damage, including paralysis and paraplegia. In a 2015 scientific publication, two scientists, Berglund and Berglund of Stockholm University, describe Shermer's Neck as follows:

> "Shermer's neck was first described in 1983 in an ultra-distance cyclist and it is often associated with neck pain (in our patient diplopia as first symptom) and exhaustion and impaired neck motor function with inability to extend the neck against gravity. The diplopia, for the first time described in connection with Shermer's neck, was accentuated when elevating the eyes and looking at distance, most likely reflecting exhaustion in the elevator muscles of the eye. Shermer's neck usually appears after 800 km of non-stop bike racing. Risk factors include

former neck injuries, staying low in aerobars for a long time, and wearing helmet light/cameras. Prevention includes neck strength training, muscle stretching, raising of handle bars and different kinds of chin support. The most important treatment is rest and not riding a bike. In our patient the diplopia was normalized after 4 hours of sleep. It can take 2-14 days to regain full neck motor function. The possibility of developing Shermer's neck and diplopia (»Berglund's diplopia«) must be taken into account when many untrained individuals participate in popular shorter races over about 300 km."[81]

Michael Shermer was one of the first Race Across America participants in 1982. In his second attempt, he had to give up because of the neck problems just described, and the phenomenon was named after him.

Due to Shermer's Neck in 2017, Patric Grüner from Tyrol, Austria had to end the race in position two about 1200 kilometers before the finish. In an interview on MeinBezirk.at, he said when asked if he himself had already guessed that the race would soon be over for him:

"I suspected it the last night, where I rode 100 kilometers to the RV with my head propped up in my hand and one-handed. That's when I realized the shit was hitting the fan. I slept in the motel for two hours, hoping it would get better. My crew then rebuilt the bike for me: a self-construction that I can put my head on. But it was no use, just like the neck brace or a cushion on which I could rest my head. I even smashed my lips open three times. Also, to hang down a counterweight behind, had no more sense. I quickly changed the bike again and realized that it was getting really critical. It was really bad when I rode towards a stop sign at an intersection and no longer looked left when turning right. In addition, I could only see 10 to 15 meters. That's when I knew I couldn't go any further ... I couldn't hold my head up anymore. No one knew what would have happened to the nerves in my neck if I had continued. Later I was told I had pretty much exhausted that problem."

Shermer's Neck also appeared on RAAM participants in 2022. Without exchanging a word with them, you can tell by the creative constructions they wear to stabilize their heads. In 2019, for example, I had seen a participant who had torn off a fence rail somewhere, which he attached to his back and tied with a loop to his chin. This construction was to hold his chin. Others mounted Pringles cans on their handlebars to rest their chin on.

Alberto Blanco with Shermer's Neck at RAAM 2011 - he made it to fourth place. (Photo: Vic Armijo)

In preparation, I had therefore done everything to avoid Shermer's Neck during the race. I strengthened my neck muscles with EMS training. South Tyrolean RAAM finisher Martin Bergmeister gave me the valuable tip of training with lead weights in my bike helmet. Another special neck training I learned from the bobsledders, who are exposed to enormous centrifugal forces in the ice channel I could experience that once myself bobsledding in the Olympian ice channel in Innsbruck Igls, in the curves I could hardly keep my head straight in the bob. A good exercise for me was to loop a theraband under both hands and around my head in push-up position, then lift my head several times to strengthen my neck muscles. This was very effective. Now, during the race, all we could do was try to get the problem under control by massaging. Especially Zoli, Alex, Ruth and Liane did their utmost.

It showed once again how well prepared we were and how efficient we were in our processes. Every short break ran strictly according to protocol and checklists. I was massaged at every stop. There are many photos of me sitting in a camping chair, just eating or drinking something and being worked on my muscles by three crew members. Riding the time trial bike was over for now though, the extreme aero position was just too taxing on the neck. With the extreme wind conditions in Kansas, the time trial bike would have been out of the question anyway.

One of the countless bridges. (Photo: Ruth Brandstätter)

We had finally arrived at the daily routine of RAAM, and it was going quite well despite my pain - if only there hadn't been that terrible crosswind. According to my plan, I was supposed to ride the 500-kilometer stage from Montezuma/Dodge City to Fort Scott, Kansas at just under 27 kph. But this average speed was impossible to reach in the given conditions.

More and more often I now met other RAAM riders. We overtook each other again and again. For me it was frightening and reassuring at the same time to see in which terrible condition they were partly! Sunburned, chapped lips, hoarse voice. If I spoke to them briefly during an overtaking manoeuvre, their biggest problems immediately became apparent. Some of them had to turn their whole upper body toward me if they wanted to look at me. Their neck muscles no longer played along. Others looked at me with swollen faces and eyes - or better, they looked through me. Others had no desire at all, or perhaps no more energy for conversation. It was frightening that they had not even completed half of the race and already seemed to be at the end of their rope. Compared to them, I felt relatively fresh. So my sleep strategy was slowly taking effect.

But I also kept fighting against microsleep, especially at the beginning and end of each stage. In Iola, Kansas, about 70 kilometers before my next stage destination, another break was planned. Bob informed me that the Rotary Club was waiting for me there. Of course, we stopped briefly, since many Rotary Clubs along the way were donating to our polio eradication project. There were some Rotarians there who welcomed me warmly and at the same time did not really know how to deal with me. By now I had cycled well over 2500 kilometers, was visibly tired and had to try very hard to exchange a few friendly words. I sat in my camping chair, got iced Coke, and we took a few photos. The break took a little longer than planned, and a glance at the clock told me that we had lost quite a bit of time that day. The wind was just too strong, and the temperature was always around 40 degrees Celsius. I would have preferred to check into a hotel here for my break, and only continue after that. I asked Bob to negotiate with our crew chief about this option. However, Zoli had no mercy on me. We had to go on.

Ruth recorded in the Facebook diary:

"After every high comes a low ... and he has to go through that. Kurt delivered a sensational performance on the bike, had a lot of fun today, but now he was mentally in a very difficult phase. He did not even want to finish the planned stage 😟. Of course he didn't get permission from his crew chief Zoltán Bogdán and his doctor Alexandra Podpeskar, although he tried it with all means. He lost the fight and is cycling now 😊 🚴 because tomorrow RAAMbazamba #stage7 is waiting and it won't be easier 😑."

On the last kilometers to Fort Scott, I fought fatigue harder than ever before in this race. I had now been on the road for 23 hours and almost 500 kilometers and could only move as if in a trance. From behind I suddenly heard a heavy honking. I was startled, looked back, then forward, and saw that I was on the wrong side of the road. There was a car in the opposite lane, thank God still coming towards me at a safe distance! For my crew and me, this moment of shock was another important lesson. We had to be much more careful from now on. Microsleep on the bike simply could not happen to us! But the incident also showed me that my crew were very alert and took good care of me.

When I finally arrived at the hotel, Hubert was standing at the entrance: "Super Kurt, fourth place!", he said.

I can't remember if it was because of my limited perceptiveness, but eventually I thought it was a joke. Until then, I had had no idea what position I was in. I didn't want to know either, because

I was racing for myself and our fundraising project, sticking to my strategy and not wanting to be influenced by other race participants at all. Somehow, however, this statement kept me busy. Could this be true? I had indeed overtaken cyclists again and again!

Day 7 - Sleep deprivation

Today we were supposed to leave Kansas behind us. The stage was relatively short with 400 kilometers and 2600 meters of climbing and was intended more for regeneration. But there was not much to recover, even this short stage demanded everything from me. With each passing day it became more and more difficult for me to become awake and alert after the sleep break, and I found the first two hours to be pure torture. I fought fatigue with every means at my disposal. The most effective was listening to cabaret. The Austrian cabaret artists Josef Hader and Michael Niavarani not only helped me not to fall asleep in the first two or three hours after the sleep break, but they noticeably improved my mood. Either their pieces were played to me through the loudspeaker mounted on the support vehicle or I listened to them through the headphones in my right ear (according to the rules, you can only wear headphones in your right ear).

You can't train sleep deprivation - incorporating it into training is pointless. It would rather have the opposite effect, you reduce regeneration, and that would have negative consequences for the following training sessions.[82] In preparation, therefore, you couldn't do much more than think about the right sleep strategy and a few tactics for staying awake.

Months before the start, I therefore began to completely avoid caffeine. In cycling, caffeine is not only a means of increasing performance; on the long haul, it is indispensable as a wake-up agent.[83] The effect of caffeine on sleep deprivation was scientifically tested during the U.S. Navy Seals' Hell Week: " Hell Week consists of 5 1/2 days of cold, wet, brutally difficult operational training on fewer than four hours of sleep. Hell Week tests physical endurance, mental toughness, pain and cold tolerance, teamwork, attitude, and your ability to perform work under high physical and mental stress, and sleep deprivation. Above all, it tests determination and desire. On average, only 25% of SEAL candidates make it through Hell Week, the toughest training in the U.S. Military. It is often the greatest achievement of their lives, and with it comes the realization that they can do 20X more than they ever thought possible. It is a defining moment that they reach back to when in combat. They know that they will never, ever quit, or let a teammate down"[84] In this study, soldiers were given either a placebo or 100/200/300 mg of caffeine after training for 72 hours without sleep. Sleep deprivation reduced performance and mood, but caffeine counteracted this. Dosages of 200 and 300 mg significantly increased visual alertness, reaction speed, and physical alertness.[85] However, the effect of caffeine wears off with regular consumption, so I opted for caffeine withdrawal.

When I felt I could no longer control my need for sleep, I allowed myself a short power nap of no more than 15 minutes.

For this, my support vehicle was adapted within two minutes. There was a soft mat and cushion in each car, and I was able to rest well - even in the greatest heat - in the air-conditioned van.

We had copied another remedy for microsleep from the bodybuilders - smelling salts: "Inhaling concentrated ammonia through the nose irritates the nerve endings in the nasal mucosa. This causes a reflexive movement - away from the odor and perhaps the formation of tears. Further, it can activate the sympathetic nervous system, leading to what's called the 'fight-or-flight' response, which puts us on alert."[86] The body reacts with a mild panic response, breathing and heart rate may accelerate, oxygen transport to the brain may increase, and thus performance may increase. This all sounded convincing to me. Even though the few scientific studies on this tend to assume a placebo effect, smelling salts were extremely effective for me. Just a quick sniff and I was wide awake again!

Not only because of the dangerous incident the day before, I now took the problem of sleep deprivation very seriously. In the history of RAAM, there have been two deaths so far. In the first, Brett Malin was killed in a collision with a truck. The second death occurred in 2005, when Bob Breedlove died in a collision with an oncoming vehicle. This happened near Trinidad, after the Rocky Mountains. At that time he was riding alone, his support vehicle far behind him. The cause of the accident has not been fully clarified, but microsleep is considered very likely. Austrian RAAM participant Alex Gepp arrived at the scene of the accident immediately afterwards. After the Rocky Mountains, he was just on the long descent towards Kansas: "At the end of the descent, however, we are abruptly stopped. What looks like a construction site at first glance turns out to be a traffic accident after a few meters. I am slowly guided past the scene of the accident by a police officer. There is only one vehicle to be seen, which was probably involved in the accident. It doesn't even look badly damaged ... Only after the RAAM will I learn the sad news ... Dr. Bob Breedlove gets into the oncoming lane on a downhill near West, about 40 kilometers before the Time Station in Trinidad, probably caused by a microsleep. Bob is alone on the slightly sloping road at the time, as his crew is currently supporting him via leapfrog. An approaching driver of a pickup truck is unable to react in time and the collision has serious consequences. The 53-year-old Iowa physician is killed instantly."[87]

As long as the body is in motion and active, the risk of microsleep is relatively low. However, the monotony on the long straights and especially lying on the aerobars significantly increase the risk. Above all, however, it's the downhill sections where you have to be careful as hell not to be overcome by fatigue.

The ability to concentrate waned continuously as the race went on. From time to time, I already had difficulty calculating how long I would need for a certain distance at a given average speed. When someone from the support vehicle spoke to me, it often took me what felt like an eternity to find the right answer. I had known beforehand that this would happen. That's why we had agreed before the race that I would delegate all decisions to my crew on the starting line. In such a state, it was no longer possible to think rationally. The only decision I still made myself was when I needed a toilet break.

I can't remember the exact moment, but sometime in the last third of the race I had my first hallucination. It was night time, and I was driving along a road that was littered with asphalt cracks that had been repaired with grout. From this, the most beautiful works of art were created in my mind on the road. The cracks turned into pictures. The road workers left messages, they painted hearts on the road, wrote something in Arabic script, and once I could clearly recognize the cartoon characters Max and Moritz and the widow Bolte. A day or two later - this was already towards the end of the race - large, dangerous eyes stared at me from the roadside. At least every 100 meters I felt pierced by their gazes. Then, in a bright moment, I realized that they had been mailboxes. Hallucinations are a well-known consequence of sleep deprivation. Paranoia, anxiety, depressed mood, and increased risk-taking are added to the mix.

This stage from Fort Scott in Kansas to Washington in Missouri became much more difficult than I had expected. My favorite bike, the white Venge, had a defect again. A broken headset had to be repaired! Probably it had been the hard hits on the road with the cross joints in Colorado that had strained the ball bearing. Again, I had to switch to my old spare bike. My riding position on this bike, however, was not set up for riding with aerobars and was therefore far from ideal. But could I do? I had to go on.

That day I met more often the Frenchman Christian Maudit. We had arrived at a Time Station at the same time. He was sitting there, without shoes, and made quite a battered impression. His feet were in a terrible condition. Swollen, the toes stained blue-black - he must have been riding in terrible pain.

In the meantime, a group of a few riders was close together in the race: the Danes Peter Skovbak and Søren Peter Rosenkilde, the Indian Kabir Rachure, Phil Fox, Les Crooks and Jim Trout from the USA, and Jeff Spencer from Great Britain. Riding was now much more fun than the days before. Again and again, a foreign crew vehicle stood at the side of the road and cheered me on. Especially at night, that was incredibly motivating. The atmosphere among the race participants and within the crews was good, people helped each other when someone needed something and motivated each other.

At the next crew change after sunrise, my team had a special surprise for me. Someone gave me a smartphone and played a video. Six-time Race Across America winner and record holder Christoph Strasser had sent me a video message! I could hardly believe it, and his message was a real motivational kick for me:

> "Hello, dear Kurt and dear crew. I'm busy training myself right now, but of course I'm following the Race Across America as best I can, and for once I'd like to express a big compliment and my greatest respect. How you are on the road! Above all, what really inspires me is the smart strategy, having the courage to take more breaks - even at the beginning - maybe to fall behind a bit, but also to sleep

during the day in the big heat. I think that was really a good decision, and it seems to be paying off now in the second half of the race. You're catching up, you have even more power than the others, and I hope it continues so well. I'm keeping my fingers crossed for you. You know the track. That's your big advantage. You know you've done the heat in the desert, the thin air at the height of the Rocky Mountains, windy Kansas. But now, in the last third across the Mississippi River, it's going to be difficult again. Very difficult, in fact. Lots of elevation gain in the Rolling Hills, the steep Appalachians, but you'll make it. Stay strong. All the best and love from Romania."

Christoph Strasser's video message. (Photo: Christoph Strasser)

My crew witnessed how much the motivational messages inspired me and now knew how they got me back on the bike, especially in the difficult phases! From now on, I should be regularly presented such video messages!

In Jefferson City, a small Missouri town named for Thomas Jefferson, the third American president, we made a 15-minute stop right in front of the Capitol. It wasn't a minute before two Rotarians approached us. They had been following the race and were waiting for me! We exchanged a few words, took a photo, and moved on.

The character of the race changed now, it led increasingly through populated areas, which meant more variety. From time to time, but far too rarely, spectators stood at the side of the road, cheered me on and applauded. Even car drivers occasionally greeted me.

There were still about 125 kilometers to go before the next sleep break in Washington, Missouri. Again, this stretch held a new challenge. Saddle sores! I was still on the spare bike and switched to my Tarmac from time to time, but it didn't have aerobars mounted on it. After all, it was intended for the mountains. With difficulty and with great pain I reached the hotel. There my Venge was waiting for me, the RAAMbler Car had been able to have it repaired in Washington, Missouri. Thank God.

Leadership Lesson 7: Find your individual strategy

The finisher rate at the Race Across America is less than 50 percent. Fewer than 30 percent of the rookies, i.e. those taking part for the first time, finish. 2021 was a particularly tough year due to weather conditions: of the twelve solo starters, only three made it to Annapolis. 2022 was also a difficult year: of the 33 solo starters, only 14 made it, representing a 42.5 percent finisher rate.

I set myself a clear goal for my RAAM. I wanted to finish safely - not as a zombie, but as a human being, and I wanted to have a "once-in-a-lifetime experience" with my crew, have fun and - as far as possible - enjoy the race. The classic strategy of most RAAM participants was therefore out of the question for me. My strategy was fundamentally different from the typical approach.

I knew that the race would not be won with my strategy - but that was not my goal. The sleep breaks would be much too long for that, I would lose too much time. My reasoning, however, was that with my long rest periods I could avoid many of the big problems (sleep deprivation, Shermer's Neck, saddle sores, total exhaustion, mental weaknesses). My hope was also that the long sleep breaks in the hotels would allow me to regenerate better. True, I would fall far behind in the first few days - perhaps even finishing last by a wide margin. But I was sure that in the second part of the race I would have more strength and energy and above all more mental fitness and thus could make up some time.

My strategy	The "classic" strategy
• 4-5 hours of break per day (5 minutes break every three hours, 15 minutes break every nine hours).	• As short "standing times" as possible; every minute you don't ride is lost time that can't be recaptured
• 2-3 hours sleep per day	• As little sleep as possible, short power naps
• Sleep breaks for me and my crew in the hotel, no motorhome	• A motorhome as a constant companion and for the sleep breaks
• Sleep break over midday, when it is hottest	• Sleep breaks mostly at night
• First sleep break already after 24 hours	• First sleep break as late as possible, usually after 36 hours
• Nutrition almost exclusively through high-calorie liquid food	• Varies: from pure liquid food (e.g. Christoph Strasser) to "eat what you can tolerate and what tastes good".

My strategy worked. At the end of my first stage (Time Station 5 in Salome) I was in fourth place. In front of me were the favorite Rainer Steinberger, the multiple world champion in ultracycling, Nicole Reist, and the Australian Alan Jefferson (who eventually won the race). Due to my early and long sleep break at the beginning I was far behind. After my start in Salome, I was in 25th place. In Tuba City, Time Station 10, I was in 13th place. Then in Trinidad (Time Station 20) I was 10th. During the race I slowly but steadily caught up. My strategy was successful. I finished third in my category and stood on the podium of the Race Across America, next to the

Australian Alan Jefferson and the US-American Jim Trout! I finished sixth overall! As an underdog, I was mixing in the world class of ultracycling.

Time Station	Placement
TS 5: Salome	25.
TS 10: Tuba City	13.
TS 20: Trinidad	10.
TS 30: Fort Scott	9.
TS 45: West Union	9.
TS 55: Finish in Annapolis	6. (3rd in Master Class)

How did I manage to achieve this top ranking with my unconventional strategy? Michael Porter, strategy professor at Harvard University, offers a simple definition of strategy: strategy is about being different. Strategy is about deliberately choosing a different set of activities to create unique value propositions![88] This is compelling, but sounds simpler than it is. In practice, we observe the opposite. Instead of differentiating themselves from others, companies' strategies are becoming increasingly similar. The culprit is a phenomenon known from sociology: isomorphism.[89] We describe this phenomenon in detail in our book "Open Strategy"[90]:

"Isomorphic" sounds fancy, but it just means "similar in form." And we human beings are, it turns out, pretty similar in form to one another in some surprising ways. Take our behavior. As studies of eating habits have revealed, obesity is contagious[91].4 If your friends are overweight, you will likely be as well[92]. When light eaters hang around heavy eaters, they tend to eat more, and the reverse also holds true. To lose weight, don't pay all that money to Weight Watchers (now WW). Just start having dinner with friends who aren't all that enamored of food! Other behaviors are contagious, too. Teenage girls are more likely to become pregnant if they see their friends having babies. Kids earn better grades if they're surrounded by friends who are strong students. And here's an interesting one: when two people live together, they eventually start to look alike. In part that might reflect your and your roomie's similar eating habits, but it also owes to your tendency to imitate one another's facial expressions[93]. "Humans are not exactly lemmings," Richard Thaler and Cass Sunstein write in their book Nudge, "but they are easily influenced by the statements and deed of others … If you see a movie scene in which people are smiling, you are more likely to smile yourself (whether or not the movie is funny); yawns are contagious, too." [94]

There are several reasons for this: First, only the best business models survive (survival of the fittest); second, we tend to copy success models; and third, people within an industry often have similar backgrounds (e.g., education, experience, etc.) that make us think alike.[95] Often, therefore, what is needed are outsiders who look at things differently, unblinkered and without blinders, and who have the courage to do things completely differently.

Read the story of Vivek Ranadivé, the basketball coach who led his daughter's basketball team to success - with a very unconventional strategy. Malcolm Gladwell describes it in his book "David and Goliath: Underdogs, Misfits and the Art of

Battling Giants[96], and in our book "Open Strategy"[97] we use the example to illustrate how outsiders can break with tradition and win with new rules of the game using very unconventional strategies.

When Mumbai-born Vivek Ranadivé, who grew up watching cricket and soccer, first saw a basketball game, he thought it was pretty pointless. When one team scored a basket, it would immediately retreat to its own end of the court and wait there patiently for the opposing team to bring the ball in, dribble to the other side, and then - probably - score. This process repeated itself throughout the game. This pattern can be observed in almost every game - isomorphism at its best. Basketball has clear rules. It is played on a court that is about 90 feet long and 50 feet wide, the top of the 18-inch basket is exactly ten feet off the floor. There are five players on each team, and the game is played in four quarters of twelve minutes (NBA). Following several rules, the team that throws the ball through the opponent's basket more often wins. These rules of the game lead to typical strategies and tactics. Generally, a good team had great players, good dribblers, good shooters and good tactics. When Ranadivé decided to coach his daughter's middle school basketball team in Redwood City, he realized that this group of twelve-year-old girls "was not your conventional winning team. The girls didn't come from athletic families. They weren't tall or well coordinated. They couldn't shoot. They were underdogs but we turned that to our advantage.."[98] So how could you build a successful team? Looking back on his successful years coaching this team, Ranadivé says:

"Underdogs have to think outside the box. They can't rely on size and strength. We had to think more strategically and find unorthodox approaches to the game. We analyzed our opponents' weaknesses and found most teams, immediately after scoring, retreat to defend their basket, giving their opponent the opportunity to inbound the ball to their teammate without pressure and execute a well-practiced play with precision.... Lacking much skill, but we had to disrupt that flow. We had to play in real time. We had to play a full-court press, the entire game. By taking the unconventional approach, we were able to catch our opponents off-guard, which gave us the advantage. And we won, a lot." [99]

There are two important rules that led Vivek Ranadivé to this strategy. First, when one team scores a basket, the other team has five seconds to put the ball in. Second, the team has ten seconds to move the ball across midcourt. Redwood City's Ranadivè team did not retreat after scoring. The girls shadowed very closely their opponents and were mostly successful in preventing the opposing team from bringing the ball in within five seconds. Either a player panicked and threw the ball away, or the Redwood City girls intercepted it. And when the opposing team successfully played the inbounds pass, the girl who caught the ball was immediately attacked, so she couldn't get it over the middle of the field within ten seconds. With this strategy, the Redwood City team caught their opponents cold.

The strategy was so successful that the team made it to the U.S. Championships. A terrific achievement. From time to time, other teams tried to copy this strategy, but it never caught on. Why? Under uncertainty, we tend to copy successful competitors. It's often far too risky for us to go down unconventional paths.

We can learn two lessons from this story. First: As an underdog, you can hardly compete in the world class if you try to copy the strategy of the champions one-to-one. I had the impression that many RAAM participants try to copy the success strategy of Christoph Strasser and other record winners. But what works for Strasser doesn't necessarily work for everyone else. As an underdog, it makes little sense to copy the strategy of the champions, because they have perfected it for themselves and adapted it to their individual strengths and needs. It's worth thinking about how you can do things quite differently. And secondly, it often takes an outsider who sees things quite differently and then also has the courage to choose a different strategy.

Day 8 - Saddle pain

During the sleep break, Alex examined my seat more closely. The top layer of skin had peeled off, which was not yet a big problem. However, individual superficial inflammations of the hair follicle were visible, which - due to bacteria - can develop into abscesses. We had already paid attention to hygiene and care during the whole race and tried to prevent such a development at all costs. But now it became serious. Open sores in the seat area are not only very painful, but also carry the risk of blood poisoning. Not infrequently, participants have had to end their race for this reason, including a RAAM rider from Switzerland this year. He was doing very well in terms of time, but initially developed neck problems (Shermer's Neck), which he managed to get under control again. However, his seat problems were so massive that he had to give up. He happened to be in the same hotel in Annapolis as we were. When he told us about it, my team doctor suggested that she examines and treats him. He must have suffered terribly, she just said.

Despite all the difficulties: The mood is good!

After the sleep break, I got on a cleanly cleaned and perfectly serviced bike, as usual. Balázs' effort was great. He was not only a reliable driver and mechanic, he took care of my bikes, and in his calm manner he contributed significantly to calmness, especially in difficult situations. With stoic composure he endured my whims when the saddle height had to be changed, the inclination of the saddle adjusted, the pedals readjusted and the sticky bottle cage cleaned. Time and again I found something that didn't suit me. Balázs endured my whims with enormous patience.

Soon after the start in Washington, Missouri, one of the very big highlights was waiting for us: the Mississippi. He who crosses the Mississippi reaches the destination, so they say. After the Mississippi bridge at Saint Louis, it was only another 1500 kilometers! I still had more than four days to do it. The goal was getting closer. If nothing worse happened, if no unexpected health problems arose, I would actually reach Annapolis!

The saddle sores worsened, however, and the pain was sometimes unbearable. I therefore rode a lot standing up and changed my sitting position again and again to find a spot on the saddle that didn't hurt. Again and again I tightened my cycling shorts. In advance I had already done everything to avoid this problem: I had the bikes perfectly adjusted to me, and I had tested so many different saddles until I found the right one for me. In the end, there were eight of them in my garage. I had also compared cycling bibs from nine different manufacturers.

To avoid pressure points, I had different bibs with different paddings to change. I also had bibs in smaller sizes with me. Valerio Zamboni, a RAAM legend from Italy, once lost so much weight during the race that his bibs became too big, and chafed his skin. I even carried padded cycling underpants and a large, soft women's saddle. If nothing else had been bearable - I could still have sat on it somehow. So I was well prepared, and also during the race we did everything to prevent seat problems. I changed bibs every eight to nine hours. Especially in the heat, sweat could cause salt crystals to build up in the padding, chafing the skin. Good hygiene was crucial. We had a detailed protocol for this as well, and Florian in particular adhered to it mercilessly. At every pee break, he stood behind me armed with disinfectant spray and chamois cream and insisted that I follow his instructions. My crew was tasked with reminding me every 15 minutes to stand up for a minute if I didn't do it on my own. This was to relieve pressure on my sitting area. At every intersection and stop sign, I was reminded to stretch my neck, and my crew reminded me to stretch my hands at least once an hour to prevent carpal tunnel syndrome. We had also thought about problems with our feet. Permanent pressure on the same spot can also cause numbness in the feet. I had specially made insoles and several pairs of different cycling shoes with me, which I changed every eight to nine hours.

Alex now turned his attention to my saddle sores. Painkilling and numbing cream brought, albeit only partially, some relief. Antibiotic ointment should prevent inflammation. From Jefferson City on, I could only tolerate one particular pair of bibs, the ones of my cycling team Physio 1.0. Thank God I had seven of them with me! Somehow we also got the seat pain fixed. Nothing escalated. But we were aware of the danger of a chain reaction - because as a cyclist you tend to ride standing up more when you have uncontrolled saddle sores, you shift the pressure points to your hands and feet and put a lot more strain on your knees. So, a seat problem can very quickly lead to numerous other complaints.

When we crossed the Mississippi, the mood improved abruptly! I could feel how happy the entire team was and how everyone had the feeling of certainty that we would reach the finish line. That made us temporarily forget the exertions of the race.

The rest of this day's stage was rather unspectacular. Relatively flat it went through Illinois and Indiana, but still with very high temperatures close to 40 degrees. Florian and Martin wrote in the race diary:

> "The Girls team took over from 9:45 and led Kurt through Illinois, where he really flew at times. However, since the leg would last well into the night, saving energy is all the more important. The American team takes over from 5:30 p.m. and leads Kurt into the night, where they hand off responsibility to crew chief Zoli and his team, who leads Kurt to the hotel for a sleep break at 3:30 a.m. in Bloomington, Indiana. A Brazilian four-man team passed Kurt during the night - and celebrated him as if he were at 'Carnival in Rio,' giving him an eerie boost."

Leadership Lesson 8: Solve problems while they're small

In 1969, Stanford University psychologist Philip Zimbardo reported on a series of experiments he conducted in New York and in California.[100] He positioned a car without license plates with the hood open on a street in the Bronx in New York and a comparable car on a street in Palo Alto, California. The abandoned car in the Bronx was attacked by "vandals" within ten minutes. The first to arrive were a family - father, mother and young son - who took the radiator and battery. Within 24 hours, virtually everything of value had been removed. Then the random destruction began - windows were smashed, parts torn off, upholstery ripped. Children began to use the car as a playground. Most of the adult "vandals" were well-dressed, apparently well-groomed whites. The Palo Alto car stood untouched for more than a week. Then Zimbardo himself smashed part of it with a sledgehammer. Soon, passers-by joined in. Within hours, the car was upside down and completely destroyed. Again, the "vandals" seemed to be primarily respected whites. With these experiments, Zimbardo tested a phenomenon that became known as the "Broken Windows Theory". This theory describes why a single broken window of an abandoned building can lead to vandalism and decay of an entire neighbourhood. If a broken window is not repaired immediately, it does not take long for another window to be broken. This then results in a chain reaction: an unrepaired window is a signal that no one cares, and it costs you nothing to break more windows.[101] If nothing is done about minor offenses like breaking a window, graffiti, public urination, trash lying around, etc., it quickly leads to vandalism and decay. The lessons learned? Problems need to be solved while they are still small. For policing, for example, this means that police officers should not only focus on major crimes, but that police patrols and foot patrols can be very effective because they can prevent minor offenses, thereby avoiding escalations like the Broken Windows phenomenon.

The most common reasons for a DNF at RAAM include Shermer's Neck, saddle sores, and the consequences of sleep deprivation. None of these problems come unannounced. They develop slowly, and it is critical to be alert, interpret the first signals correctly, and act immediately. For example, if you ignore the first signs of saddle sores, you risk them getting out of control and leading to a chain reaction. If you can no longer sit because of pain, you ride more standing up. Riding more while standing puts more stress on knees and hands. Knee problems and carpal tunnel syndrome are then often the result.

Already after a few days I felt my neck. We reacted immediately to the first signs of Shermer's Neck: I got neck massages at every three-hour break, and I gave up the time trial bike, which with its extreme aero position puts a lot of strain on the neck. We also took the first signs of saddle sores very seriously, we reacted quickly with all the necessary measures: special hygiene, disinfection, antibacterial creams, change of bibs, change of bike, etc. My doctor constantly monitored the development. None of the typical problems escalated, we always had everything under control. I crossed the finish line in comparatively good health.

The reason for this was that

> 1) we had thought out well in advance what the first weak signals were for all sorts of problems to watch out for,
>
> 2) we were especially vigilant and did not ignore any of these signals,
>
> 3) we reacted while the problems were still small enough to be easily controlled.

Day 9 - Motivation

From now on it became really tough. I got to feel the hardship of RAAM with all its force: knee pain, sleep deprivation, and seat pain. But I had expected it and had to deal with it. The race diary said:

> "After - according to doctor Alexandra - a good sleep during the early morning hours, Kurt starts at eight o'clock into the stage to Athens in Ohio. Just at the beginning, however, he seems a bit battered and tired today. He has problems concentrating into the afternoon, and the day is a real challenge for him and also his support team at the beginning. During this phase, he is also unable to make up places as in previous days and remains in ninth

place for the time being. Two short power naps and a somewhat longer sleep break at the Oxford time station in Ohio bring Kurt back into the game. Above all, the cooler temperatures in the late afternoon and at night allow him to regain his old strength, and he is back in eighth place at midnight. The American support team writes at 23:30: 'He doesn't want to stop earlier, he's so motivated!'"

My support team had already been very busy for a few days to keep me in a good mood. And they all came up with a lot for my motivation. The girls in the RAAMbulance car had a different motto for each day, with which they surprised me. Once in a hippie look, once as cowgirls, once in leather pants and once - this inspired me especially - dressed up as nurses in miniskirts. The RAAMbler team motivated me with music, brain teasers, information about the course of the race and constantly tried to stay in contact with me. They read me Facebook comments and motivational messages from friends and often from people I didn't even know but who were following the race.

Othmar Peer, the well-known sports presenter and connoisseur of the cycling scene, once left the following Facebook entry:

> "If I'm honest - I get sick when I think about what Kurt still has to master. We like to call ourselves competitive athletes (I don't like hobby athletes so much), but what these athletes have to achieve at the RAAM degrades us to hobby athletes again, so to speak. My utmost respect - no matter how this story ends. And the same goes for the

support team. If someone thinks that the support at RAAM is a vacation in the States, he has no idea what kind of stress and demands the crew has to deal with. In Tyrolean – "a wild story" (a wilde Gschicht) for all involved! All the best - friends! Othmar Peer"

The RAAMedia Car was now with me constantly. Martin and Hubert passed me again and again, they stood at the side of the road, filmed and cheered me on and were also there during the breaks. They couldn't have gotten much sleep either. The RAAMerica team now unpacked the motivational posters: "Pedal now, whine later!" could be read on one of them, for example. They had already prepared these posters at home. Darlene, orderly as she is, had attached a flow chart to the back seat of the car for this purpose. Each poster had a title, a sequential number, she had thought about where and when which poster should be shown and sorted the motivational posters accordingly in ascending order. How well prepared she was!

Knee pain, seat pain and a permanent need for sleep were now my constant companions. I had to realize that my strength in my hands was diminishing somewhat. When you're in the middle of a race, it's actually not *that* bad. You get used to it, it's everyday Race Across America and it's part of it. You focus on the moment when everything will be over and bear everything that may come until then with patience. In retrospect, now with a few months' distance, it was unimaginable torture. Nevertheless, not everything was an ordeal. There were always wonderful moments - full moon in the desert, sunrise in the

Rocky Mountains after a night of rain, sunrise in Monument Valley, even the second part of Kansas with its wide, green, slightly hilly meadows was beautiful. Being able to experience all this with my team made up for everything.

My crew had found an important key to my motivation. Whenever I was feeling particularly bad - usually in the first two to three hours after sleep break, between 2 and 5 in the morning, or in the last two hours before sleep break - they would come up with a new motivational video. They moved the mountains to cheer me on: Ski legends Franz Klammer, Hans Knauss, Niki Hosp, Benni Raich and Marlies Schild cheered me on. I received video messages from the governor of Tyrol, Günther Platter, and from winemaker Leo Hillinger. Former Austrian pro cyclist Thomas Rohregger, Tour de France winner Andy Schleck and Italian pro cyclist Matteo Trentin greeted me via video. My Rotary Club Innsbruck Goldenes Dachl rewrote the song "We Are Family" and turned it into a motivational song. Julia and Irene played air guitar for me, and Christian from the Physio 1.0 Cycling Team even unpacked his poetry skills. Whenever we could, we sent back a short video with a thank you. Srini Gokulnath, the first Indian finisher of RAAM, kept sending me video messages, and Tyrolean RAAM finisher Wolfi Mader reminded me in one of his videos what was actually going on here:

> "Hi Kurt, thank you so much for your nice video that I just got sent to me from your team. I actually just wanted to tell you very briefly: Are you really aware of what you are

doing right now? Just to give you a quick reminder: That's ten times the route Innsbruck-Vienna plus twenty times the Großglockner. It's the Race Around Austria twice in a row without a break in between. It is 50% more than the complete Tour de France including 10 to 20% more altitude meters. But they take three weeks to do it and are highly paid professionals, have rest breaks in between, have a peloton and can draft ... It's twenty times the Ötztaler Radmarathon in terms of distance, and ten times the Ötztaler in terms of altitude. That's something you have to keep in mind the closer you get to the finish ... You'll be one of the very, very few who have passed the toughest sports test in the world that you can possibly do. That's an effort you get to feel. All the exhaustion, pain and fatigue that you feel until you reach the finish line is a normal condition - for you and for a RAAM finisher - because you are trained for it and made for it and prepared for it. But it is completely abnormal for 99.99% of humanity. The only thing that will not be lost from you until the finish is your morale, is your unbroken will. The will to finish, the will to finish. No matter what happens ... You will have to endure all sorts of things, but no one and nothing can break your will. And as I observe, you have an incredible will. Only people with the will to reach the goal, with the intelligence to set the right goals, with the right strategy, the right preparation, the right team can do it. Everything has worked well so far and everything will be fine the coming miles to the finish line. You're over the Mississippi Bridge. A RAAM racer who has crossed the

Mississippi Bridge will finish! 90% of all RAAM participants who cross that bridge finish, and that's how it will be for you. I'm really looking forward to it and having a beer with you afterwards!"

From Andy Schleck, winner of the 2010 Tour de France, I got this message:

"Hi Kurt. This is Andy Schleck from Luxembourg. Believe me I know the pain and suffering you are going through now, but believe me the pain will go away, but the memory will stay forever. Certainly, the cause for which you are doing it is very, very honorable - all my deepest respect! I used to say that people who are doing the RAAM are crazy. You might be crazy, but you are doing it for the best cause you can imagine. You have my deepest respect and you have my full support from Luxembourg. Keep fighting the wind, keep fighting the climbs, keep fighting the heat, the cold in the mountains, you will survive it and certainly for the cause you are doing it people will remember you. Good luck!"

The cohesion of the crew was incredible. We had now been on the road for nine days and over 4000 kilometers. Neither heat, rain, cold, sleep deprivation nor technical breakdowns could do us any harm. On the contrary, I had the feeling that my crew became more motivated, more committed and even stronger with every problem they solved. There was nothing they couldn't get to grips with. It was all up to me. I had to get to the finish line, if only for my great crew!

But there were still over 1000 kilometers ahead of me. During the day it was still hot and humid, the nights were already getting cooler. This stage from Bloomington, Indiana, to Athens, Ohio, was difficult enough with 450 kilometers and 2650 meters of altitude, but the real endurance test of RAAM was still ahead of me: the Appalachian Mountains. So I had to manage my strength very well, and I tried not to let three or four other RAAM participants, who now had about the same rhythm as me, throw me off my game. Again and again we racers overtook each other. That brought a lot of variety into this day, and the hours flew by.

Except for a short detour in the middle of the night, it remained a quiet race day. This detour, however, had it all. When we got to where it started, I stopped because the road was closed. Not only was it the middle of the night, but it was also the middle of nowhere. I had no idea where to go now. Bill got out of the car and explained to me that it was off to the left - a few miles down a deep dirt road! That can't be! Uphill! Since it was time for a five-minute break anyway, Darlene prepared the camp chair and I dropped into it. A car with searchlights now came from behind and had us in its sights. It approached, stopped a few feet away, and a sheriff got out. He asked what we were doing here in the middle of the night in this godforsaken area. Bob explained the situation, and the sheriff just shook his head, "Race Across America - you guys are crazy!" We had him reassure us again that this dirt road was taking us in the right direction. He looked at me, then at my bike and said, "Yeah, good luck, my boy!"

At RAAM, of course, you always have encounters with law enforcement officers. Especially at night, a flashing, slow-moving or roadside escort vehicle can seem suspicious. At the Racer Meeting before the start, the organizers also point out time and again that police officers usually can't take a joke and that you have to strictly follow their instructions. If you drive a car in the USA, you should know that there are a few important rules to follow during traffic controls: the police car stops at the rear of your own car, the policeman usually approaches with his hand on the gun, your own hands are to be placed on the steering wheel, under no circumstances should you get out of the car without being asked to - this is interpreted as an escape attempt, and under no circumstances should you look for papers in the glove compartment without being asked to - this could be misunderstood as an attempt to bring out a gun. All in all, one should behave passively, address the police officer as "Sir" or "Officer" etc. When our media team left Durango, in the Rocky Mountains, in the middle of the night to get shots of me at Wolf Creek Pass, it was raining hard. Martin and Hubert accelerated their big SUV a bit over-motivated to get to the pass on time. It didn't take a minute until their car was flooded by the red-blue flashing light of a police patrol. It was now a matter of pulling over to the right-hand side of the road as quickly as possible, putting on a guilty expression and recalling a phrase of apology from their experiences with Austrian and German police officers. But all this was not necessary at all. The policeman was very courteous and friendly and simply said, "I know you're with a RAAM team and want to meet your athlete. It's dark, it's raining and you were going too fast. Slow down a bit, you'll catch the cyclist. I wish you all the best and good luck!"

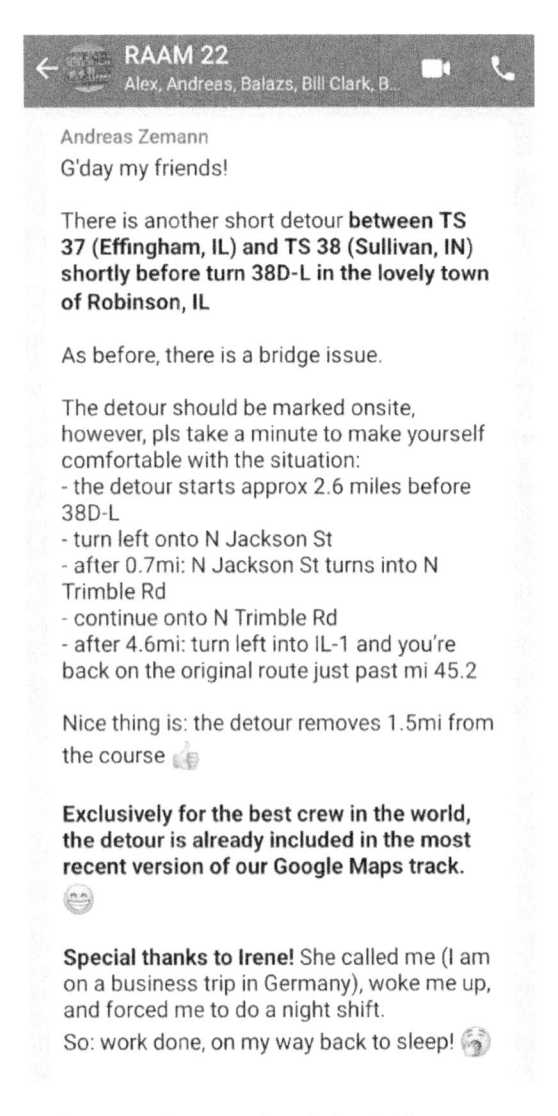

> **RAAM 22**
> Alex, Andreas, Balazs, Bill Clark, B...
>
> Andreas Zemann
> G'day my friends!
>
> There is another short detour **between TS 37 (Effingham, IL) and TS 38 (Sullivan, IN) shortly before turn 38D-L in the lovely town of Robinson, IL**
>
> As before, there is a bridge issue.
>
> The detour should be marked onsite, however, pls take a minute to make yourself comfortable with the situation:
> - the detour starts approx 2.6 miles before 38D-L
> - turn left onto N Jackson St
> - after 0.7mi: N Jackson St turns into N Trimble Rd
> - continue onto N Trimble Rd
> - after 4.6mi: turn left into IL-1 and you're back on the original route just past mi 45.2
>
> Nice thing is: the detour removes 1.5mi from the course 👍
>
> **Exclusively for the best crew in the world, the detour is already included in the most recent version of our Google Maps track.** 😁
>
> **Special thanks to Irene!** She called me (I am on a business trip in Germany), woke me up, and forced me to do a night shift.
> So: work done, on my way back to sleep! 🌙

Andi and Irene plan our detours in night shifts.

An encounter that will be remembered. Most police officers know about RAAM, and when a team combines it with a charity project, it is especially respected - at least that was our experience during several encounters we had with police officers.

When we started a few minutes later, I realized what the policeman had meant by "Good luck". It went first a few minutes uphill, then a little longer - thank God not too steep - downhill and then another felt eternity on a gravel road through forest and meadows, until we were back on the normal route. The gravel road was the purest horror. A few years ago I was with the Karbonritterrunde (a group of Austrian cyclists around Joe Margreiter and Thomas Rohregger) on the road bike from Innsbruck, Austria to Saint-Tropez, France. We crossed the Colle delle Finestre, a famous Giro d'Italia route with a few hundred meters of elevation gain on a gravel road. I thought I therefore had enough experience with the road bike on gravel roads, but this surpassed everything. Deep, very rough gravel, in which my wheels sank again and again, and I had to watch like hell that my handlebars did not twist. I was afraid for my wheels and for the frame, because again and again stones splashed in all directions, and I was afraid to fall. It was pitch black. I don't remember how long I was on this gravel road at walking pace, but it must have been at least an hour.

When we turned back onto the normal route - it was already well past midnight - I asked for a jacket. It had become cold.

"No jacket," was Bill's response.

No jacket? Something had gone wrong with the crew change! The box with my warm clothes was in another car. Bill gave me an undershirt he could still find and I put it on over my jersey. It was still about two hours until the next crew change, so I had to hold out that long.

We were in Ohio by now, the RAAMbler team had taken over, and until Athens, my next sleep break, the constant ups and downs in this hilly landscape were giving me a hard time. The night had turned cold and foggy, and from a quiet country road I was now on a highway with lots of morning traffic. The first rays of sunshine warmed me up a bit, and I was looking forward to a hot shower and two or three hours of sleep at my hotel in Athens.

In the Facebook diary, Ruth summed up the day this way:

"When the going gets tough... 😖 Now it gets really tough. The fight against the remaining kilometers, the headwind, the constant extreme fatigue and the increasingly steep climbs of the Appalachians starting in Ohio begin to take their toll. Kurt cycles on, however, undeterred 💪 The signs of fatigue are slowly making themselves felt not only in Kurt, but also in his crew. Suddenly, small deviations from the daily routine appear to be major challenges 😓 But we are a strong team, the atmosphere is excellent, everyone sticks together, everyone gives their best, everyone has a common goal ... To get Kurt to Annapolis healthy. And our team doctor Alexandra Podpeskar, who takes care of Kurt almost around the clock, is next to him, our heroine 😍.... because ... yes ... we do this together 😍.

A very special thanks today to Scott and Lisi, who have warmly greeted us on the track and provided us with power food 😍. We also send our love to you Alexandra Xandi Meixner. Kurt will cycle through the night today, only in the morning in the sleep break, so that he is then ready to rock the Appalachians 🚴 🏃.

#RAAMbazamba 😊

Day 10 - The hardest part of RAAM

I woke up with knee pain, and today it was particularly severe. Cramped, I lay in bed with gasping breath and moaned loudly in pain. As usual, Alex was with me the entire sleep break, taking care of my knees. It was around noon, and my crew was already ready to leave. In the hallway outside, I heard voices. Ruth and Liane were talking to each other. Ruth asked Liane to see how I was doing.

"I can't do this," Ruth said. For her, my pain was a great burden.

Somehow I managed to get out of bed, somehow I managed to get dressed, and somehow my crew got me on the bike after about 20 minutes. This time was always especially hard, and Alex wouldn't let me out of her sight. She wouldn't even let me go to the bathroom alone, the risk was too great that, dazed as I was, I'd fall over somewhere. From the hotel room to the bike that was kept ready for me, I was supported. Step by step, slowly and silently, almost as if on the way to the guillotine. Only with the difference that the suffering does not have an end, but the torment starts all over again.

Only 775 kilometers to go. It was Friday, June 24, around noon. I still had a whole three days until the finish line. I knew that if nothing worse happened, it would turn out. But I also knew what would wait for me over the next two days. Today's stage took us through West Virginia to Cumberland, Maryland: 380 kilometers with 5,000 meters of elevation gain, much of it on busy Highway 50.

Highway 50. (Photo: Ruth Brandstätter)

The routebook says it all about this section of the route:

"TS 44 to TS 45 Athens, OH to West Union, WV.

The terrain moderates for the rest of Ohio but once into West Virginia past Parkersburg some of the most difficult climbing in RAAM begins. The altitude doesn't approach that of the Rocky Mountains but the climbs are relentless. There is more elevation gained in this section than any other time station segment anywhere east of Flagstaff but the most difficult measured in feet of climbing per mile ridden is still ahead between Cumberland and Hancock in Maryland.

TS 45 to TS 46 West Union, WV to Grafton, WV

Endless rollers. Traffic in Clarksburg is very heavy: the excursion south of US 50 avoids most of it but involves some tricky navigation on often poorly maintained two lane roads. After crossing I-79 (mile 47) US 50 narrows to an undivided 2-lane road but remains busy."

The coming section was characterized by relentless climbs, never-ending rolling hills, heavy traffic on the highway, poor road conditions and an extremely difficult route to navigate! In comparison, the deserts, the Rocky Mountains and the Great Plains had been pure pleasure. After more than 4000 kilometers in nine days, now came not only the most difficult section of the route, but also the most dangerous. All RAAM participants were already suffering from massive sleep deprivation and concentration problems here. I knew the route. Already in the years before we had asked ourselves again and again, why one exposes the cyclists to such a risk and sends them on this highway. Not infrequently in RAAM history, there had also been accidents here. In 2018, a large SUV had crashed from behind into a support vehicle that was supposed to accompany and shield the cyclist. There were serious injuries. This year, too, there was a similar accident. It caught the Dane Peter Skovbak. His follow vehicle was hit from behind by another car and he also crashed. Fortunately, no one was seriously injured, but the car and bikes were so badly damaged that he had to give up about 700 kilometers before the finish.

> **Race Across America**
> 1 Std.
>
> PETER SKOVBAK OUT AFTER VEHICLE IMPACT
> JUNE 25, 2022 1:00am EDT
>
> Peter Skovbak has withdrawn from RAAM. The following is a statement from his crew about what happened.
>
> RAAM Media Two corresponded with crew chief, and former RAAM solo finisher, Andy Christensen, who confirmed that everyone involved in the crash is okay and will fully recover. No word yet on whether Peter plans to return in th... Mehr anzeigen
> Übersetzung anzeigen
>
> **Peter Skovbak - Team Next Step**
> Folgen
> 8 Std.
>
> Das ist ein paar Stunden nach unserem Unfall. Unser Begleitwagen wurde von hinten angefahren und diesbezüglich auch Peter angefahren und in den Asphalt verbrannt. Alle 3 im Auto und Peter wurden zur Kontrolle ins Krankenhaus gebracht und es geht den Umständen entsprechend gut und alle werden voraussichtlich zu 100% gesund

Message from the race organizers about Peter Skovbak's accident.

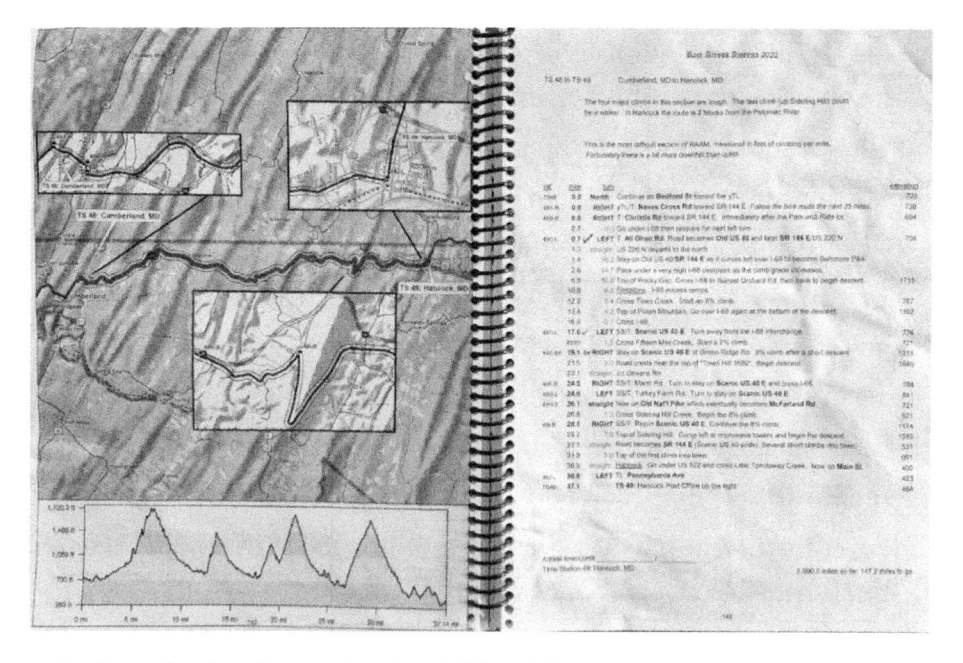

The Routebook - the navigation bible of the RAAM.

I remembered a similar situation we had experienced in Kansas in 2019. I was on my time trial bike, with my support vehicle behind me. Andi and Irene were standing on the right side of the road filming. I rode by and was happy to get a nice film shot. I was already at least 200 meters away when a truck approached from behind. Andi still held the camera on it, zoomed in and filmed how the truck came dangerously close to us. It made no move to change to the passing lane. Suddenly, the brakes squealed and the tires smoked. At the last second, the truck driver noticed us and applied the emergency brakes. It's hard to imagine what could have happened. It wasn't until we got home that Andi showed us these pictures.

I had a queasy feeling on this highway. Imagine that with us in Europe: On the highway, an follow vehicle with cyclists driving at a speed of 10 km/h during the climbs, and trucks and cars overtaking on the left at over 100 km/h! On the highway, one tries to stay on the emergency lane as much as possible, in order not to be a dangerous obstacle for heavy traffic together with the escort vehicle. However, this emergency lane is in a glaringly bad condition - it is littered with holes, shredded tires, garbage, pebbles, broken glass. In contrast, it is still comparatively harmless on the roadway. The rumble strips at the edge of the road, which are supposed to remind drivers rudely that they are coming to the edge of the road, need a lot of attention. These rumble strips can be very dangerous for the cyclist, especially if you don't have a firm grip on your handlebars. Especially when receiving drinking bottles or food from the car, you had to be very careful and not come across these rumble strips under any circumstances.

I had to make this experience in 2017. I had been on the road with my time trial bike. The road leads over countless climbs with 100 to 200 meters of altitude, and of course you try to use the short descents afterwards to take as much momentum as possible for the next hill. In aero position, lying on the aerobars, I was speeding down the highway at over 60 km/h along the emergency lane when I had to dodge an obstacle to the left, went over the rumble strips, which banged the bike and me so hard that my handlebars broke downward. It all happened in a split second, so I can't even remember how I managed to stay in the saddle and come to a stop unscathed. The shock was deep. A fall at 60 km/h can have fatal consequences. I can't imagine what would have happened if I had hit the road in this traffic!

So we had another tough day ahead of us. Not only for me - for my crew it was pure stress. They had to shield me from behind, permanently keep an eye on the rear view mirror, navigate me once or twice across several lanes on the highway to the left to turnoffs, protect me from the vehicles coming from behind, find suitable places for a break on the highway, etc.

We now had about 160 kilometers ahead of us on Highway 50, but despite all these adverse conditions, I was looking forward to it! I knew that once we had this behind us, we could tick off another big chunk. We were in our daily routine: three hours of riding, five minutes of rest. The traffic was heavy, as expected. It was humid, and my fatigue was becoming a problem. I had trouble concentrating, at times barely avoiding holes in the road.

The RAAMbulance car with the girls accompanied me. We were all nervous. Liane was behind the wheel and did a great job. She had driven the entire route up to here, and in Annapolis she will be the only driver in our crew who has driven the car every single meter of the 3000 miles. Up to 15 hours a day - a strong performance. Liane did a great job. Over time, a silent but precise communication had developed between me and my team in the support vehicle, which was of particular importance along this section. With every briefly indicated sideways glance or delayed kick, my crew knew immediately how to react, and pans to both sides could thus be made exactly in sync to give maximum safety.

The breaks on the highway were a real challenge. Twice we had no choice but to simply stop on the breakdown lane, set up the camping chair next to the car and hope that we were visible enough!

Short break on Highway 50, penultimate day of racing. (Photo: Ruth Brandstätter)

On one of the countless descents, I was unable to avoid a pothole in time, and I was hit so hard that my lamp was torn from its anchorage and flung onto the road. I had to stop and mount a replacement lamp. According to RAAM rules, bike lights must be on 24/7, front and back. We were on the emergency lane of the highway, and while Ruth was still getting the spare light out of the car, Alex sprinted off - she had her safety vest on, of course - and made a mad dash for the light in the middle of the highway, risking her life. Cars whizzed by to her left and right, but she was indeed successful. She came back with the light still working, mounted it on the bike and ordered, "Let's go!"

I obeyed, pedaled and tackled the next hills.

After about 160 kilometers, the exit from the highway - accompanied by "Take me home, country roads" by John Denver - finally came to West Virginia. The landscape became lovelier, and I was incredibly relieved that we had left the highway behind us. Les Crooks, Kabir Rachure, Søren Peter Rosenkilde and I were close together on this stretch of road, passing each other again and again, depending entirely on our break routines. On the way into the mountains of West Virginia, I once again saw Kabir Rachure, to whom I had already become really accustomed. Every time I passed him, his crew cheered me on. This time, Kabir was standing on the side of the road, completely exhausted and desperate. It was already dark, and his crew was feeding him. I had ridden very gently the day before, knowing that it was now down to the wire. I didn't see Kabir again after that. I also passed Les Crooks and Søren Peter Rosenkilde for the last time somewhere along this stretch. All three finished hours after me.

The 160 kilometers on the highway, the permanent up and down with the 5000 meters of altitude took their toll. The night became a horror for me. I had only one goal in mind: the hotel in Cumberland, Maryland. There a sleep break and then with last strength to Annapolis. It had become cold in the meantime, about ten degrees Celsius. During the next break, I suggested to my crew to move up the sleep break from Cumberland to McHenry. McHenry is at about 800 meters of altitude, and from there it is more or less always slightly downhill to Cumberland. We would thus shorten today's stage by about two hours, and I would be able to recover a bit. This would make the last leg a little longer, but it would start with a very easy 60-kilometer section. My crew saw how exhausted I was - and so were they. The suggestion also convinced my crew chief, and so a hotel in McHenry was booked.

The distance to that point was manageable, and with great relief I got back on the bike. As with every stage, the last kilometers were the most difficult. A few kilometers before McHenry, there was an emergency vehicle on the road. Emergency personnel were in the process of closing off the road. On top of one of the power poles - still simple tree trunks in some parts of the U.S. - was a massive firework. It hissed and smoked, and the street was brightly lit by the flying sparks. It was really scary. But more frightening than the sparking power pole was the fact that the emergency services might not let us drive on and that I would have to spend my sleep break in the car. Just in the last second we were allowed to pass the danger zone before everything was closed off. Once again we were lucky. Finally I saw the sign of McHenry. Finally! Then also some hotels followed, only ours was not to be made out. After the end of the town I stopped and wanted to know what was going on. Where is our hotel?

Darlene, Bob and Bill were also puzzled, but told me to keep going. After two or three kilometers I stopped again. Since there were no more houses to be seen, I feared I had missed the hotel. Bob got out, calmed me down, and said it was now two or three more miles. For me this was terrible. For 30 minutes I had been expecting to be in front of the hotel at any moment, and now I was supposed to pedal a few more miles? In 2022, there were still areas in the U.S. with no or very poor Internet coverage. So it was often not so easy for the crew to give accurate information about locations and distances. I rallied one last time for the day before we actually reached our stage finish after about two miles and I could take my last sleep break before Annapolis.

The final sprint

On June 25 at 5:23 a.m. I started my final stage of the Race Across America. I had 4510 kilometers and 37,200 meters of climbing behind me. In front of me lay the last 369 kilometers. I tried not to think about the 5150 meters of climbing of this last section. "This is the most difficult section of RAAM, measured in feet of climbing per mile," the routebook read. All the crew members and I were in a good mood, today we would reach the finish! Today our dream would come true. Moreover, the first 60 kilometers were easy, straight ahead or slightly downhill to Cumberland, Maryland. After that, however, the short but steep climbs in the Appalachian Mountains began. We started the day full of motivation and soon reached Cumberland. There we took a short break before tackling the climbs that were just behind each other and looked as dangerous as teeth on a saw blade in the elevation profile.

I felt ready - despite great respect for the upcoming climbs - but was then surprised at how easy they were. I felt strong, and cheered on by the girls we managed them in pretty much exactly two hours. After all, about 1000 meters of altitude and 45 kilometers. We were euphoric now. How easy this last stage was for me. There was still some up and down to the next short climb in about 50 kilometers, then another 40 kilometers rather flat before the last small mountain of the Race Across America had to be conquered. Then the last kilometers to Annapolis.

At the last of these four climbs, I saw an follow vehicle standing from a distance. Follow vehicles are easy to recognize because the warning lights mounted on the roof have to flash when in service. Behind it was a second vehicle, it looked quite like a Race Official. I felt for the RAAM participant, who - it seemed to me from a distance - was obviously going to receive a time penalty for breaking the rules. As I approached, I noticed several people standing in the street, debating vigorously. Seconds later, I recognized our RAAMbler car. Is this really true? Do we get a time penalty on the last day of the race? This was our fifth RAAM participation, and never before had we received a time penalty. We were considered an exemplary team, adhered to every rule and were always perfectly organized. The one hour time penalty didn't bother me as much as the fact that we had made a mistake. I approached the cars at walking pace. Now they were all standing on the side of the road, looking at me, and I could hear them discussing loudly - but still not understanding a word. A few meters ahead of them, I realized what was going on. They were in a great mood. The Race Official had stopped behind the RAAMbler Car to talk to my crew and cheer me on. As we passed, we high-fived, the Race Official congratulated me and yelled, "See you in Annapolis!"

There were still about 200 kilometers to go with some elevation gain when my euphoria waned and a stubborn fatigue set in. In my head, I was already at the finish line, and it was incredibly difficult for me to motivate myself for the last kilometers. I asked more and more often for a short break and needed two power naps within three hours in order not to fall asleep on the bike. It was another very hot day. It felt like these last 200 kilometers were now longer than the first 4700. The finish seemed to be getting further and further away from me. There were about eight hours to go. A piece of cake - compared to the almost eleven days we had already spent on the route. But those eight hours suddenly seemed barely manageable. No other RAAM participant was to be found far and wide, already for hours I was on the way completely alone! I knew this feeling from the Race Around Austria. 2020 I felt the same way there. The more certain you are that you will reach your goal, the harder you experience the last hours. They become an eternity, and even the best motivational tricks of the crew hardly have any effect. The following year, in August 2021, I felt quite differently on the last 100 kilometers of the Race Around Austria. A few kilometers ahead of me was Thorsten Weber, and Zoli managed to ignite my ambition. We started a hunt for him. I received an update from the crew every few minutes on where he was. I expected to see him around every bend now. Sometimes I got closer, sometimes he increased his distance - I was always informed. In the last flat section before Mondsee, I finally saw him ahead of me. I literally raced past him, but he didn't even seem to notice what was happening. On the last 100 kilometers from Bischofshofen to the finish I took a whole 50 minutes off him. What fun this chase was, how exciting and short were these last 100 kilometers. How many reserves of strength I was able to mobilize!

The memory of this situation rose up in me. At that moment, my support vehicle pulled up with the three girls. Alex leaned out and yelled, "You're in fifth place, Les Crooks is coming up behind! Step on it! Don't let him catch you! Ahead of you is Phil Fox. If he takes another nap, you'll catch him!"

That did its job. I was suddenly wide awake. Alex had pressed the right button. The fun began. The tiredness was gone. Every few minutes, I had an update given to me. I wanted to know exactly how the gap to the rear was changing. Even Andi Zemann, who was following the race from home in Telfs, Austria got involved. He is a good statistician and can calculate distances and deliver forecasts in real time. The last small hill with about 300 meters of altitude came my way and I saw here the chance to finally shake off Les Crooks and demotivate him. He should see no point at all in pursuing me any further. I pedaled really hard once again and was surprised myself how many reserves I could still mobilize. Now it was just under 100 miles to the finish. At the top I asked for an update again. Indeed

- I had increased the distance clearly. There was hardly any danger from behind. Only six hours left.

I now had to think about our 2019 RAAM finish in the four-man team. Ruth and I had taken over that night, and we had a hot duel with a four-man team from Germany. We kept overtaking each other. We had maybe 50 kilometers to go before the finish, when I waited somewhere on the side of the road to take over from Ruth. The men's team T408 from Germany passed me and we stopped the gap. Eleven minutes! They had dropped Ruth on the final hills. Eleven minutes, with the time trial bike it might work out, I thought to myself. I set off in pursuit. On the time trial bike I could be pretty fast when I needed to be. At the next red light, I received information from the support vehicle that the other team had changed tactics: all four of them were on the course - drafting! This was a common tactic at the end of a race. It allowed them to make up a few minutes in the final kilometers. I didn't get discouraged and kept going. But suddenly my gears failed. I had forgotten to change the batteries. At that moment, the traffic light in front of me turned red. I had to stop anyway and used the time to change the batteries. Of course, they could not be found immediately in the support vehicle. A whole green phase passed until I could start again. Now I was really motivated. I gave everything I could and received a message from the support vehicle that we were closing the gap - quite quickly, in fact. T408 had probably not counted on me anymore. A few kilometers before the finish we used a little trick: Ruth was sent ahead in the support vehicle and stood with her bike at the side of the road. When T408 passed her, they had to assume that we were planning another change. And since changes during the night are only allowed to take place while standing, this had to cost us two to three minutes of time. As I passed Ruth, she cheered me on. T408 had just passed. I pedaled full speed once again, but couldn't overtake them before the finish line. It was only a matter of a few seconds. The surprise came in Annapolis: we had beaten the Germans by two minutes. Since the team in Annapolis had started a few minutes ahead of us, we had a time credit! I took a whole 13 minutes off the team of four, which rode the last 50 kilometers drafting - despite my battery breakdown! This thought motivated me at that moment.

One last crew change and about 100 kilometers to go: Innsbruck-Ötztal train station and back! Less than Innsbruck-Brenner and back! An evening training lap! That's how close we were to the finish now. But we weren't there yet. I had to continue to concentrate. With a fall, everything could be over so close to the finish. The RAAMerica team took over now, and Alex switched from the RAAMbulance car to their car. As in the last few days, she stayed with me for two support shifts. The RAAMbulance Car, the RAAMedia Car and the RAAMbler Car made their way to Annapolis to wait for me at the finish.

Evening had fallen when the escort vehicle pulled up to me, the back door window opened, Alex stuck her head out and said, "I have some good news and some bad news. Which one do you want to hear first?"

I noticed how bad she felt about it and knew right away what was going on.

"The bad one," I said.

"You're not in fifth place, I made a mistake."

Alex had mistakenly assumed that Svata Bozak was no longer in the race, she had confused him with Peter Skovbak, who had to give up after 4200 kilometers due to an accident. Alex probably expected me to freak out now, and I think I surprised her quite a bit with my answer: "Doesn't matter. Fifth or sixth place ... doesn't matter. The last few hours were so awesome, it was really fun!"

"The good news is, you're third in your age category!"

It was only about 60 kilometers to Annapolis. Only two more hours! But the news from Alex did not remain without effect. The game was now over, the fun had end abruptly - suddenly the air was out. After a last short break, I got on the bike one last time to torture myself through the remaining kilometers to the finish. I knew the course well by now and knew that it would be difficult and needed a lot of concentration: a multi-lane, busy road with some traffic lights and many complicated junctions. It was awful. My tiredness was suddenly back, the goal so close to my eyes was getting further and further away from me. I could no longer find a rhythm. It had already become dark. Meter by meter I fought now. Now I had already ridden over 4800 kilometers and could not believe that the last few miles did not want to end. It seemed to me as if I was riding in slow motion.

The finish line was anything but spectacular. A tape stuck on the breakdown lane and an orange traffic cone at its end. It appears abruptly and is easy to miss. To the right of it in the green are one or two race officials. Behind it a small restaurant and a parking lot. As I crossed the finish line, the Race Officials applauded, and some patrons on the restaurant terrace clapped. Bizarre! That was the finish line.

But I was not yet a finisher of the Race Across America. I had crossed the finish line, but I was not yet at the finish! From here it was now neutralized to the City Dock in Annapolis, it was still just about ten kilometers! To the time stopped at the finish line, 26 minutes are added to each rider. This is the Race Across America - it doesn't want to end. Even after crossing the finish line, it's not over yet. The next stop for me was now the Shell Station, a gas station just before the City Dock. You had to stop there, had a few minutes to get ready to cross the finish line, and then you were escorted to the finish line by a RAAM vehicle. My entire team was waiting for me. When I arrived, cheers erupted. We fell into each other's arms, Race Officials congratulated us. I changed bibs and the jersey, we took a few photos and waited for the escort. Only two of us were missing: Zoli and Balázs. Where were they? I looked around and spotted them: hunched over my bike, each holding a cleaning rag, they were shining up my S-Works Venge. That was my crew: After 5,000 kilometers across the U.S., they were cleaning my bike: "You don't ride to the finish with a dirty bike!" was the clear message.

Now it was time to go. The last few minutes. In front of me drove the escort - a convertible. On the back seat sat Martin and filmed. Behind me, my follow vehicles. With great fanfare, with sirens and horns, we drove to the City Dock, where the big finish arch was set up. At 10:50 p.m. we were there! We were in Annapolis! We made it! Eleven days, five hours and 50 minutes. 4880 kilometers, 42,300 meters of climbing, three mountain ranges, two deserts, twelve states, four time zones, 550,000 pedal strokes, 145,000 calories, 158 liters of sweat lost. Eleven days, five hours and 50 minutes that I had spent years preparing for. Eleven days, five hours and 50 minutes in which my crew did everything for me and reached their physical and mental limits just like I did. Race Across America 2022: We were at the finish line!

At the finish line. (Photo: Florian Phleps)

Rank	Entry	TS#	Miles	Race TM	Avg	Status
1	620 - Allan Jefferson - Team Jefferson	54	3028.20	9 d 23 h 20 m	12.65	OFCL
2	300 - Jim Trout	54	3028.20	11 d 3 h 29 m	11.32	OFCL
3	654 - Kurt Matzler - Rotary RAAMs Polio	54	3028.20	11 d 5 h 50 m	11.22	OFCL
4	665 - Les Crooks	54	3028.20	11 d 7 h 57 m	11.14	OFCL
5	660 - Søren Peter Rosenkilde - Team SkyDog	54	3028.20	11 d 9 h 52 m	11.06	OFCL
6	632 - Joff Spencer Jones	54	3028.20	11 d 18 h 13 m	10.73	OFCL
	668 - Peter Skovbak - Team Next Step	44	2606.90	9 d 22 h 35 m	10.97	DNF
	644 - Peter Trachsel - Team Trachsel	38	2257.80	8 d 18 h 31 m	10.77	DNF
	642 - Paolo Pietro Godardi	34	2017.60	8 d 0 h 29 m	10.53	DNF
	635 - Lionel Poggio	33	1940.40	7 d 13 h 20 m	10.75	DNF
	664 - Adriano Ongaro	17	1020.80	4 d 6 h 40 m	10.04	DNF
	268 - Ricardo Arap	13	824.10	3 d 3 h 7 m	11.1	DNF
	634 - Chris Davies	7	445.50	1 d 22 h 36 m	9.56	DNF
	670 - Jean-Luc Perez	2	145.30	7 h 48 m	18.63	DNF
Age Cat (50-59) Count: 14						

Results list Masterclass.

After the interview on stage and a few photos, we celebrated. Ruth had bought Champagne. In Formula 1 fashion, I popped the cork and we drank from the bottle. Since there wasn't much going on at the finish line and I wasn't suitably dressed to go out, we drove to the hotel. In the lobby we had another beer or two, and then it was off to bed. That was it.

I slept surprisingly badly, after a few hours I was awake again. My crew was busy for hours bringing the cars back to their original condition, packing the bikes and getting everything ready for departure. We enjoyed another lunch together right at the harbor. Martin, Hubert and Liane flew back in the evening. We said goodbye to the Americans on Monday. We spent one more day in Washington D.C., my flight together with Ruth, Zoli and Alex left on Tuesday. My last Facebook entry in the USA:

"Hello from Washington!

I'm having a coffee in Washington D.C. right now and only slowly realizing what happened. We actually did it, and even with a top ranking and $1.2 million in donations. This was a world-class effort by an incredible team. With a very unconventional strategy, we were in the league of the world's best ultracyclists. I am overwhelmed ☺ . With the right team, you can accomplish anything. Thank you to the legendary team Rotary RAAMs Polio.

Leadership Lesson 9: Marginal gains - the sum of small improvements makes a big difference

We tend to focus on the big things and underestimate the importance of the small improvements. James Clear writes about this in his book "Atomic Habits": We often forgo small changes because they don't seem to matter much at the moment. If you save a little money now, you still won't become a millionaire. Whoever goes to the gym three days in a row is still not in shape. Whoever learns Chinese for an hour tonight still doesn't master the language. We change our behavior a little, but when the results are slow in coming, we slip back into the old rut.[102]

But once the strategy is in place, it's a matter of continuously improving the many small things: The sum of the small improvements makes the big difference!

As an example, James Clear cites the history of the British Cycling Team.[103] The team had played no role in cycling for over 100 years: it had not won a single gold medal at the Olympic Games since 1908, and not once had a Briton won the Tour de France in over 100 years. The British Cycling Team's performance was so poor that a leading bike manufacturer refused to sell the team its bikes for fear of damaging its image. Everything changed in 2003 with new sports director Dave Brailsford. In 2008, British Cycling won 60 percent of the gold medals in Beijing, and in 2012 the team set new Olympic world records in rows. Bradley Wiggins became the first Briton to win the Tour de France, and Chris Froome followed up with multiple victories. In ten years, the Brits secured 178 world championship wins and 66 Olympic and Paralympic victories. Sports director Dave Brailsford was obsessed with "Marginal Gains:" " The whole principle came from the idea that if you broke down everything you could think of that goes into riding a bike, and then improved it by 1%, you will get a significant increase when you put them all together."[104] Every single detail was studied, tested and improved: wind tunnel tests for aerodynamic racing suits, better saddles, tires were rubbed with alcohol for better grip, the optimal massage gel was sought for better muscle recovery, surgeons showed athletes how to wash hands to prevent infections, pillows and mattresses for the best sleep were tested, biofeedback sensors monitored how athletes responded to training and so on and so forth.

Christoph Strasser, equally obsessed with the idea of continuous improvement, succeeded in making history through a sum of many small optimizations in his 2021 24-hour world record attempt in Zeltweg, Austria: 1,026 kilometers in 24 hours! As Race Official, I was able to witness firsthand how he himself was surprised by his result:

> "Calculated were: For 41.67 km/h, the necessary average for 1000 km, 280-290 watts would be necessary, and I can not do that. Especially not in the aerodynamic seating position ... The result in the flatlands of Styria, Austria was: 272 watts were needed for 42.75 km/h. Pretty clear what the numerous small optimizations to the seat

position, aero setup and bike still made up. But just: unexpected.

I kept thinking to myself: Oh man, damn it, what's going on? Where's the speed coming from?

I already knew the setup was good, waxed chain, ceramic bearings, special tires from Specialized, thinner tubes, a custom time trial suit that was determined to be the fastest of many models in aero testing on the track, etc. ... But I've never tested it as a complete package in training, I've always just test ridden the individual parts. Sometimes the helmet, sometimes the suit, sometimes the disc, then the tire - to see if everything fits and the outfit is endurable at the temperatures. The chain doesn't last forever, so it's only put on before the start. With the helmet, the training is dangerous because you hear less from the surroundings, the tires are a little more susceptible to defects. Therefore, I tested everything only a little and individually, what the total package of the many small 'marginal gains' gives speed, I realized only after the starting gun.

During the ride, I was constantly calculating the average speed, how much I could lose to stay above 1000 km. And when I realized that I wasn't dropping at all and that I didn't feel like eating 110 g of carbohydrates per hour, it was clear to me that this was going to be my day.[105]

Christoph Strasser had optimized everything that could be optimized! He was obsessed with the idea of Marginal Gains!

This was also my motto for the entire preparation of my Race Across America. After each race (Race Across Italy, Race Around Austria) I sat down with my crew chief Zoli and we discussed every little detail: What can we do differently? What can we improve? We met once a week during EMS training for years. And during each training session, we philosophized about improvements. Those who are so obsessed with Marginal Gains often find quite unexpected opportunities for improvement: Christoph Strasser was once in the wind tunnel at Specialized to test aerodynamics. David Misch describes this in his book "1000/24 - Christoph Strasser and the Hunt for the Best Day":
[106]

> "The prospect of being able to measure there in the wind tunnel the loss of speed caused by the slightest changes, such as an awkwardly placed helmet, a thicker jersey fabric, or even an open front zipper, strikes his numbers- and statistics-oriented mind. When it was pointed out to him that the pleasant cooling provided by the constantly open and then wildly flapping jersey cost him more than the sinfully expensive high-profile wheels and all the other little fiddly bits added up to, he vowed never again to touch the zipper or order the jersey half a size larger. Even the position of the water bottle ... added up to minutes or hours in the calculations over the RAAM distance."

For my RAAM I tried to optimize everything. Only in the seating position did I make major compromises. At this long distance, you have to carefully weigh up aerodynamics, power transmission and comfort. I opted for more comfort because I didn't want to take any risks. But I found out many other surprising details in return: If you shave your arms, that can add up to 19 seconds over 40 kilometers - as tested in the wind tunnel.[107] Converted to the RAAM distance, that's theoretically just under 40 minutes. My S-Works Evade helmet is 50 seconds faster than a conventional road helmet, which is 80 minutes calculated over the entire course! The cleaned and properly oiled chain can make up a few watts according to tests,[108] equally effective are aerosocks, which provide small benefits. I tested countless bike saddles, bike shorts, and tweaked my riding position for months - almost every training ride - until I found the perfect one. We also kept finding ways to improve the processes during the race. At the Race Around Austria, we found that changing clothes can take a relatively long time, especially if you have to find your jersey, bibs, socks, sleeves, gloves, etc. first in the chaos in the support vehicle. Therefore, we packed individual sets of cycling clothes in little bags, sorted by desert (white clothes), rain, cold and normal conditions. This certainly didn't save more than a minute or two, twice a day. But over the entire distance, it made up maybe 20 minutes. If you add up all the tiny time savings, it adds up to hours! These hours can be crucial, as some participants just barely don't make the twelve-day cut-off!

Toto Wolff, Head of Motorsport at Mercedes, is one of the most successful motorsport bosses in Formula 1, and his team is one of the best in the world. He is a perfectionist like no other. The first time he visited the team's guest area, he complained that the toilets were not clean enough.

" That cannot be," he said at the time, " this is our home on a race weekend and where our sponsors come with their families."

He hired a hygiene manager who always accompanied the team from then on.

" I physically showed him how I wanted him to clean the toilet, how to put the brush back, how to wipe the floor, how to put the soap bottles with the front facing forward, how to sanitize the handles, and so on. And I walked him through what I wanted his schedule for the week to be, and how on Sundays, when it is busy, I want him to park himself right next to the bathroom and make sure it is spotless after every guest."

He complained that the "F 1" logo was nowhere to be seen in the reception area. When asked if it was the engineering that determined success, he replied, "No, it's the attitude. It all starts with an attention to detail!" [109]

My lesson from all this: Having the right strategy is crucial, but at least equally important are the Marginal Gains, the sum of the small improvements! If you are obsessed with the pursuit of perfection and take all the effort to learn and optimize, you can be rewarded by surprising successes!

Leadership Lesson 10: Hire for attitude, train for skills

Pete Penseyres, two-time Race Across America winner, coined the phrase, "The crew cannot win the race for you, but they can lose it!"

The crew is one of the most important factors for success. Michael Shermer, one of the four cyclists who first competed in the Race Across America in 1982, a multiple finisher of that race, and a former race director, developed a set of criteria to distinguish members of the crew:[110]

1. "Desire to crew with an urge for adventure able to rough it.
2. Able to not shower or put on make-up.
3. Able to get dirty and keep smiling.
4. Sense of humor.
5. Thoughtful to others.
6. Able to avoid arguments by biting their tongue.
7. Smart and inventive.
8. Able to maintain some semblance of hygiene even during the rough parts of the race.
9. Someone who is totally committed to the rider even if the rider does not perform to his or her own expectations.
10. Able to catch short naps and still remain alert.
11. Able to drive safely.

12. Not too verbose (silence is often golden in the support vehicles)."

The support crew not only has to look after the cyclist, navigate him, take care of logistics, do the shopping and keep in touch with the race headquarters. The crew plays a crucial role in motivating the racer - especially in the last part of the race. The racer needs medical care, physiotherapy, bike mechanics, someone who knows about electronics and cars, support staff with good organizational skills and good drivers in his team.

All these skills and qualities are important. When putting together the crew, however, I primarily made sure that the crew members were enthusiastic about the project and the idea, that they had a high degree of "compatibility", i.e. that they got along well with other people, were cooperative, helpful, trusting and empathetic, were physically resilient and kept calm in extreme situations. We spent a lot of time in selecting crew members, following the principle: "Hire for attitude, train for skills."

For my RAAM 2022 I was able to fall back on a few proven crew members, but I had to find seven new crew members. The most difficult thing was the search for a doctor. I spoke with many interested parties, but no one was found who really fit. Months went by and time was running out. My wife Ruth finally posted in the WhatsApp group of our cycling club and asked if anyone knew someone who would be eligible. Promptly I received a call from Alex.

She was like, "I really want to do this. This is such a cool project. I would love to be a part of it. But I only graduated from medical school four years ago and I'm a pediatrician now. I know it takes a different skill set, but there are still a few months to go, and I'm doing everything I can to prepare!"

I didn't know Alex - she had only recently joined our cycling club - but after a few minutes on the phone I knew she was the one. She was enthusiastic about the project and showed tremendous willingness to do whatever it took to prepare. She sounded very nice on the phone, and my intuition told me she was a good fit for the team. I immediately agreed. Alex prepared meticulously, she read academic literature, she listened to all of Christoph Strasser's "Sitzfleisch" podcasts, and she got in touch with specialists who could help her. Alex was worth her weight in gold.

When Julia, who has been in the crew once at RAAM and twice at Race Around Austria, had to cancel, Zoli suggested a replacement: Balàsz. He was a very good friend of his, and Zoli put his hand in the fire for him. I trusted Zoli. After all, it was crucial that he had crew members in his vehicle with whom he could work well. It was a good decision.

But I still needed a crew for another vehicle. Hubert, who was president of my Rotary Club at the time, offered. He was enthusiastic about the idea. I had known Hubert for many years and knew that he could be relied upon. I explained to him that it was his job to find more team members for his support vehicle. My only condition was: they had to be crew members he could rely on and with whom he could imagine working together for eleven days in a confined space under sleep deprivation and stress. What we definitely didn't need were conflicts within the crew. Some RAAM projects have already failed because of this. But what we also definitely wanted to have in our team was a good mood: Negative moods within the crew transfer very quickly to the racer, and especially in the last part of the race the crew has to do everything to motivate him - even if he's already physically at the end. Within a few days, Hubert had his team: Florian, Martin and Roland.

I was convinced that enthusiasm for the project, personal attitudes and the ability to get along well under enormous pressure and stress were decisive. Specific technical knowledge and skills are necessary, but not sufficient.

You have two options when putting together a team: You define the necessary qualifications and skills and then look for the best person for each position, or you first define the personal characteristics and then put together the team accordingly. So which is better: a team made up of stars or a star team? Mercedes motorsport boss Toto Wolff is convinced: "It is not necessarily the best individuals who win races but the team that works best together."[111] A team composed of individual superstars can fail miserably if the teamwork doesn't work. In 1992, the U.S. put together a basketball dream team for the Olympics. Some of the best players in basketball history were on it: Charles Barkley, Larry Bird, Patrick Ewing, Magic Johnson, Michael Jordan, Karl Malone and Scottie Pippen. However, putting superstars on a team does not guarantee success. In the first month of practice, the Dream Team lost spectacularly to a college team: "We just didn't know how to play together," Scottie Pippen said after the loss. It took time for the team to finally come together. The rest is history.[112] A "team of stars" composed of individual star players is not necessarily a star team.

The common practice in recruitment follows the principle of "hire for skills and train for attitudes". The only problem with this is that you cannot easily change attitudes, values and character traits of individuals.

In a study, Scott Keller and Mary Meaney asked 5,000 leaders to think about "peak experiences" as team members and to describe what constituted that peak experience. They found three key characteristics:[113]

> First, a shared belief about what the company is striving for and the team's role in achieving that goal.

> Second, interaction characterized by trust, open communication, and a willingness to engage in conflict.

> Third, an environment where team members are energized because they feel they can take risks, innovate, learn from outside ideas, and accomplish something important - often against all odds.

Accordingly, common goals, functioning cooperation and energetic team members are crucial.

Ernest Shackleton was one of the most impressive leaders of the last century. He led the Endurance expedition to the South Pole in the years from 1914 to 1917, which failed spectacularly. In January 1915, the ship, the Endurance, got stuck in the pack ice and became stranded. The ship drifted along with the ice, and months of complete darkness passed. Ernest Shackleton kept his team fit and happy with soccer games, dog races, amateur dramatics, and other activities. In October 1915, the ship gave in to the pressure of the pack ice and broke up. Food and equipment were saved, and Shackleton carried his crew to safety in three lifeboats. After months on the drifting ice, he and his crew set off in the three lifeboats toward Elephant Island. Under the most adverse conditions and temperatures as low as minus 30 degrees, they reached the island only to find that there was no help there. Shackleton selected five men to sail the 1300 kilometers to South Georgia in one of the lifeboats. From there, he launched several rescue attempts until he saved the entire crew on August 30, 1916. The crew held together until the last day and survived in the most difficult conditions. There was no revolt and hardly any major conflicts. They helped each other and persevered together. Shackleton had chosen the right men for his undertaking. In December 1913, he had begun searching for crew members for his expedition: " Men wanted for hazardous journey. Low wages, bitter cold, long hours of complete darkness. Safe return doubtful. Honour and recognition in event of success"[114] - this is how the ad is said to have read. 5000 men are said to have applied, which the expedition leader divided into the categories "Crazy", "Hopeless" and "Possible". He met with the "Possibles" and selected based on character traits such as optimism, sense of humor, and perseverance. Character traits were equally important to him as abilities!

Nancy Kohen, a professor at Harvard Business School, studied this expedition in detail and Ernest Shackleton as a leader. She concluded:

> "Shackleton understood that in the life-threatening conditions of the Antarctic, he needed people with optimism, perseverance, cohesion, adaptability, a sense of humour, and dedication to mission. Shackleton had hundreds—perhaps thousands—of applicants to choose from, and he accepted and rejected men based largely on these attributes, always looking to create an ensemble of crew members: an integrated cast of personalities, traits, and strengths that would work well together under conditions of great uncertainty and high stakes. Leaders today can learn from the importance Shackleton placed on assembling his team and how he did this. In ongoing crises, resumes tell us less about the right fit between a person and a position than attitude and character. Hiring your team is more than filling individual positions; you are trying to build a whole that is greater than the sum of its parts."[115]

"Hire for attitude, train for skills!" Team Rotary RAAMs Polio was not a team of stars, it was a star team. Half of the crew members were not even road cyclists. The team was a team of great personalities. The enthusiasm for the project and the big goal bonded us together and made us perform at our best.

Team Rotary RAAMs Polio - the crew

The RAAMbulance Team

Ruth, my wife, had been to the Race Across America three times as a team rider and this time she switched to the role of companion. She was already a great support to me during all the preparations. How much of the organizational work she did and solved in the background without me noticing! She kept a lot away from me so that I could concentrate on the training and the race. During the race, Ruth was not only a great crew member, but also our social media manager. She kept a race diary on Facebook, kept in touch with friends and fans, and took care of endless details. As my wife, some situations must have been almost unbearable for her. To see how I suffered, endured pain and was completely exhausted. Together with Alex and Liane, however, she continuously motivated me to persevere and surprised me with cheerleader interludes that made me laugh at every possible opportunity despite the tough everyday racing life.

Alex, my team doctor, provided so much more than I could have ever hoped for. In addition to her continuous medical care, she also supported me mentally, which was crucial for the success of our project. Always in a good mood and professional, she looked after me almost around the clock. Alex slept almost as little as I did during the entire race. She hardly let me out of her sight and, especially as the race progressed, she didn't switch to a recovery break after her shift, but to the next support vehicle. I felt safe in her hands, and her calm, pleasant manner contributed significantly to my not losing faith in our goal even in the most difficult situations. I am very grateful that Alex gave her time to our project, I could not have imagined a better team doctor.

Liane joined the team at the last moment - about two weeks before the start of the race. She is a close friend of Ruth and me. We know her so well that we knew she would be a great asset to the team, even though she had never been present at a crew meeting during the preparation period. Highly organized, conscientious, resilient and up for any kind of fun, Liane provided efficiency, balance and good humor. She was the driver of this support vehicle and was at the wheel for the entire 5000 kilometers - up to 15 hours a day! Liane and I were soon communicating without having to exchange words. She interpreted every little signal from me correctly, knew what I needed even before I expressed the desire, and on the road we harmonized. She made me feel safe even on the highways.

The RAAMerica Team

Without Bob, the founder of Team Rotary RAAMs Polio, my solo participation in RAAM would never have happened. When he brought me onto the team in 2016, a new phase of my life began. RAAM and the fundraising project were with me for many years. Bob changed my life. During the race, he was sacrificially there for me. Even toward the end, when exhaustion was the daily routine for all of us, he radiated calm. Team Rotary RAAMs Polio became his big project. With his four successful participations as a team rider, our solo participation in 2022, and the more than four million dollars in donations the team has raised since 2016, Bob is the initiator of an extraordinarily successful charity project of which he can be justifiably very proud.

Bob and Darlene were irreplaceable in the preparation. They invested endless amounts of time in the planning, the organization and in the fundraising project. Darlene, Bob's wife, was both the heart and soul of our RAAM endeavor. In her kind, motherly way, she cared for the entire team. I hardly know anyone who is as organized and as conscientious and disciplined in her approach to things as she is. Darlene is the one who keeps our RAAM family - as she calls it - together and spoiled us all with her homemade "powercakes" during the race.

Bill has also been part of the Rotary RAAMs Polio team since 2016 and is incredibly experienced in his role as crew member. He always knew exactly what to do and what was important. He was usually in the passenger seat, navigating and providing me with everything I needed, taking care of me and my bike during breaks. Nothing could happen to upset him. "Are you okay?" he must have asked me hundreds of times during the race. Darlene, Bob and Bill were a perfect team and they harmonized wonderfully.

The RAAMbler Team

Zoli, Florian and Balàsz took over the night shift during the entire race - and thus probably the most difficult task. They were rewarded again and again with the most beautiful sunrises in the desert, in Monument Valley, in the mountains and in the lowlands.

Zoli was my crew chief. Together we developed the strategy and planned all the processes and tasks for the crew members. As my EMS coach for many years and companion at several races, he knew my strengths and weaknesses very well. At the starting line, I had handed over all the decisions to my crew, and Zoli thus took over the overall responsibility. He decided on the race tactics, the breaks, organized the crew and communicated with the race headquarters. He had to make many difficult decisions and was always right with his knowledge and intuition. Zoli also hardly slept more than I did. He was always there, always available and responsive to everyone. Despite his sleep deficit and despite many a hectic situation, he always kept his cool and led the team and me safely and confidently to the finish.

Balàsz has been Zoli's friend and confidant since childhood, and for this very reason we were sure that he would become an important member of our team. Balàsz was an great team player and took care of me and the bikes with the utmost concentration and composure, never losing his cool. When I was totally exhausted and distressed, he would title me "champion" or "gentleman," and before I had a chance to make known my despair, frustration, or anger over mishaps or problems, he would wave me off reassuringly and the situation would relax on its own. Characters like Balàsz, who never lose their nerve even in the most difficult circumstances and complete their tasks with 100 percent reliability, are irreplaceable in the Race Across America.

Florian was also irreplaceable in our crew. Meticulously precise, optimally organized and strictly following protocol, he looked after me through the entire night shift. Florian played a decisive role in ensuring that none of my health problems escalated at any time. During the night, he never let me out of his sight for a minute, and so I always felt safe. Without our conversations, trivial-pursuit games, or reading Facebook messages aloud, riding in the long hours of darkness would have been unbearable for me. Even in the most difficult situations, he was never unruffled. In the team, he spread "good vibes," always had an open ear when someone wasn't feeling well, and in stressful situations he knew how to put everything into perspective at the right moment.

The RAAMMedia Team

Hubert, Martin and Roland were the good-mood makers - despite never-ending workdays. It felt like they were on the set 24 hours a day. At any time of the day or night, they appeared out of nowhere, spreading good vibes and had an unbelievable feeling for shots and the right timing. Once they finally had their story, they usually had to spend hours reworking and, despite a poor Internet connection, broadcast the footage across the Atlantic in their hotel so that Martin Böckle from sports channel K19 could make the final cut and broadcast it at 5 a.m. on the dot. There were many situations in which the media team was a lifesaver for me: when they suddenly appeared with the spare bike on the second day of the race, took care of the repairs to the defective wheels, emerged from the fog in the middle of the night on Wolf Creek Pass in the rain and cold, or were simply there towards the end of the race. Martin was the gentleman, Hubert always found the right words, and Roland always had a good saying on his lips - too bad that he could only be there until Wichita in Kansas.

With us for months before the RAAM and during the RAAM on every inch of the course were Andi with Irene and Julia. As multiple crew members of our relay team at RAAM and Race Around Austria, they were an integral part of our Team Rotary RAAMs Polio. Although they could not actually be present in 2022, they looked after us almost day and night from Austria. Andi and Irene meticulously took care of spontaneous route changes and put in night shifts when necessary to adjust our navigation in time. Julia was also definitely missing from the team. With her videos and her Facebook messages, she and Irene managed to be far away, but still with us.

Leadership Lesson 11: Work hard, but plan for sufficient regeneration

An astonishing number of executives work too much and sleep too little. 38 percent of executives in Germany say they work between 40 and 50 hours a week, 27 percent between 50 and 60 hours, 4.6 percent between 60 and 70 hours and one percent work over 70 hours a week.[116] Around three quarters of executives also take work home with them in their minds - late into the night. Thirty-seven percent of respondents in a major executive study put their switched-on smartphone next to the bed, and 43 percent say they have a fundamentally hard time switching off from work.[117] Professor Curt Diehm, Medical Director of the Max Grundig Clinic near Baden-Baden, who conducted the study, says:

> "It's obvious that the modern work style of being online around the clock robs many executives of their inner peace. Those who deal with professional issues late into the night and shortly after getting up in the morning inevitably find it harder to switch off, which is, however, necessary for a deep and longer sleep."[118]

CEOs work even more hours. Michael Porter and Nitin Nohria from Harvard University studied the daily routines of CEOs in detail and came up with an average daily working time of around ten hours and, with work on the weekend, 62.5 hours per week.[119] Add to that the hours spent mentally grappling with work in their free time because they can't switch off, and it becomes quite a lot. "Among many top managers, politicians and celebrities, there is a persistent belief that little sleep means more productivity - and that this then leads to more success,"[120] reads in an article about sleep habits of top managers. Some CEOs boast about their workload. Apple CEO Tim Cook, for example, likes to be described as an insomniac workaholic.[121] His alarm clock rings at 3:45 a.m. every day. Elon Musk works at least as much: "There were times when, some weeks ... I haven't counted exactly, but I would just sort of sleep for a few hours, work, sleep for a few hours, work, seven days a week. Some of those days must have been 120 hours or something nutty."[122] According to an international study by the Center for Creative Leadership, 42 percent of executives sleep only six hours or less. [123]

Managers who suffer from a lack of sleep are not particularly good leaders. Sleep researcher Charles Czeisler from Harvard University puts it in a nutshell:

> "Tired managers act like drunks ... Otherwise intelligent and well-mannered managers behave differently when they are overtired: They berate their employees, make unwise decisions that affect their company's future, and give confused presentations to their colleagues, customers, the press, or shareholders."[124]

However, it has long been known among top athletes and sports scientists that recovery and sleep are crucial factors for success. In their book "The Power of Full Engagement"[125], Jim Loehr and Tony Schwartz hold that the true secret of peak performance is alternation between stress (energy consumption) and recovery (energy renewal); they call it oscillation. The real enemy of peak performance is not stress; rather, it is the impetus for growth. The problem is lack of recovery: "Chronic stress without recovery depletes energy reserves, leads to burnout and breakdown, and ultimately undermines performance. Rituals that promote oscillation-rhythmic stress and recovery-are the second component of high performance."[126] The key to peak physical performance lies in the principle of supercompensation. After a training load, the body not only establishes readiness to perform at the same level again, but after sufficient recovery, increases performance beyond the original level. The decisive factor, therefore, is regeneration. In strength training, for example, the muscle is stressed until fibers are actually injured. With sufficient recovery time, the muscle not only heals, it actually gets stronger. However, if you train without regeneration, this leads to acute and chronic damage. [127]

Regeneration is therefore a fixed component of every training plan. In training and sports science, this is called periodization.[128] In the microcycle, light and heavy training units alternate. Training breaks are planned in. For me, for example, there was one day a week off from training. In the mesocycle, three to four intense training weeks are followed by an easy week. Many top athletes take about a four-week training break once a year, during which they either train lightly or do other light sports. For me, this is always the month of November, when cycling outside is no longer fun and there is still too little snow for ski touring.

Too much work and too little rest are bad for your performance. John Pencavel of Stanford University found in a study that productivity per hour drops sharply when we work more than 50 hours. After 55 hours, productivity drops so massively that more hours would be pointless. Those who work up to 70 hours a week only accomplish the same amount of work as those who put in 55 hours.[129]

We know from creativity research that good ideas rarely arise in stressful situations. Teresa Amabile, a professor at Harvard University, believes that stress is a real creativity killer: On days when we work under time pressure, we develop 45 percent fewer creative ideas than on relaxed days. [130]

Another study looked at where employees get the best ideas. The results are astonishing, but I bet that reflects your personal experience pretty well: 28 percent of the best ideas come from nature, 14 percent from home, 13 percent from vacation and travel. Only then comes a response category related to work: Only eleven percent of ideas come to you on business trips and while driving to and from work. [131]

These observations are easy to explain. Ideas arise when we have free space, when we can give our thoughts free rein. This does not happen under time pressure. Nor does it happen when we are too focused on something. There are two systems in our mind:[132] once an evolutionary old system. It is associative, automatic, unconscious, parallel and fast. It processes large amounts of information. Next to it there is a second, evolutionary later developed system. It is rule-based, controlled, conscious, serial, and it is slow. This second system is only capable of processing a limited amount of information. In this context, the Dutch psychologist Ap Dijksterhuis speaks of conscious and unconscious thinking.[133] Creative problem solving needs an incubation period. An initial phase of conscious thinking is followed by a phase of unconscious thinking. Although we do not think about the problem during this phase, creative solutions still emerge. [134]

The phenomenon is familiar to all of us: We work hard on a problem, are unable to solve it, push it aside, do something else, and after an incubation period we suddenly have an "aha" moment. In his experiments, Ap Dijksterhuis investigated whether unconscious thinking helps us find creative solutions to problems. His finding:

> "The findings reported here speak to the relevance of unconscious thought in general and to the relation between unconscious thought and creativity or divergent thinking. One could say that unconscious thought is more "liberal" than conscious thought and leads to the generation of items or ideas that are less obvious, less accessible and more creative. Upon being confronted with a task that requires a certain degree of creativity, it

pays off to delegate the labor of thinking to the unconscious mind."[135]

So when we're not thinking in a task-oriented, conscious way, the most interesting "aha" moments can occur.

Do you remember Archimedes and the golden crown? He had the task of finding out whether the king's crown was made of real gold. An easy task for him. The specific gravity gave him the answer. He just had to know what the weight and volume of the crown were. Weighing the crown was easy. However, he gritted his teeth on the calculation of the volume, as he was not allowed to destroy the crown. One day, when he was taking a bath - thinking of nothing - and the water overflowed, he had an aha moment. He jumped out of the bathtub, ran naked through the village and shouted, "Eureka! Eureka!" By displacing the water, he was able to determine the volume of the crown.

So when you have difficult problems to solve and you're stuck, do something different for a change. Take a break, think about nothing. During this incubation period, your subconscious, divergent thinking processes a whole lot of information and connects dots that weren't previously connected. "Insights from the subconscious," Stulberg and Magness write, "rise to the surface only when we turn off the conscious mind and put it into a dormant state."[136]

Jim Loehr and Tony Schwartz summarize very well what you can learn from top athletes to better manage your energy. Based on their years of work with top athletes, they assume that managers - if they want to deliver top performance over a longer period of time - need to develop similar behavioral patterns as top athletes.[137]

- Healthy diet: Do not eat large portions three times a day, but eat slightly smaller portions five to six times to provide the body with sufficient energy, otherwise the body goes on the back burner and the metabolism slows down. Every day should start with breakfast, and the diet must be balanced (50-60% complex carbohydrates, 25-35% protein and 20-35% fat - especially unsaturated fatty acids). Reduce sugar in particular. Fast-acting carbohydrates such as sugar cause blood glucose levels to rise and fall quickly, resulting in a correspondingly rapid drop in performance. Also make sure you drink enough water.
- Exercise regularly (consult your doctor): three to four times a week cardiovascular training for about 30 minutes, twice a week intervals - short intense sessions with appropriate recovery.
- Make sure you get restful sleep: Sleep is one of the most important success factors in sports[138] and is also considered a performance killer in management.[139] Maintain as regular a sleep rhythm as possible with routines for falling asleep (e.g. reading a book), avoid late dinners, alcohol, and intense physical activity in the evening - these factors negatively affect your sleep

quality. Also avoid blue light (especially smartphone and tablet) before bedtime - it has an impact on melatonin production. If you have a sports watch, use it to monitor your sleep quality - you will get insightful findings. Make sure you get enough sleep - seven to nine hours. Sleep allows us to consolidate and store memories, process emotional experiences, replenish glucose (the molecule that fuels our brains), and clear beta-amyloid (the waste product that accumulates in Alzheimer's patients and disrupts cognitive activity).[140] Sleep deficit can have a dramatic effect. Staying awake longer than 18 hours decreases your reaction time, short- and long-term memory, concentration and decision-making skills, computational power, decision-making speed and spatial orientation suffer.[141] Staying awake for 17 to 19 hours is the same impairment as someone who has 0.05 per mille of alcohol in their blood. 28 hours without sleep equals 0.1 per mille of alcohol.[142]

- Schedule recovery periods every 90 to 120 minutes: Chronobiologists have found that the body's hormone, glucose and blood sugar levels drop about every 90 minutes. Without recovery periods, your performance suffers. Even short breaks are enough for significant recovery. Use these breaks to eat, drink, exercise, and for mental and emotional variety.[143] If your schedule doesn't allow for regular breaks, take advantage of a sports watch to schedule your day. For example, with the help of my sports watch, I've found that there are activities at my job that lower my stress level enough that I regenerate while doing them. When I'm writing - on a book or on a scientific paper - I often get into a flow state. I forget everything around me and lose track of time. My stress level drops, and my "body battery" recharges! I regenerate while working!

Scott Behson, professor of management, says, "From a management standpoint, we need to rethink the notion that non-performance time is wasted time. Instead, we need to see that recovery is a key component of sustained high performance. This means we must resist continually increasing the time demands we put on our employees and expecting our employees to be constantly "on call" even after hours. We need to encourage our employees to take lunch breaks, relax on weekends, and actually take their vacation days, unplugged (and also do these things ourselves). By helping to strike the right balances, we can build the work-life athleticism we need when the stakes are highest."[144]

1.2 million for polio eradication

Since 2016, the Rotary RAAMs Polio team has been raising funds to eradicate polio. Since then, more than four million dollars have been raised, and about 1.2 million in 2022 alone. Polio (poliomyelitis, or polio for short) is a highly contagious infectious disease of the nerve cells of the spinal cord, caused by enteroviruses. While in many people the infection proceeds without symptoms or only with mild symptoms, one in about 200 infected persons develops symptoms of paralysis: "The symptoms of paralysis set in later and usually begin in the legs. As the disease progresses, they can spread to the arms and eventually to the respiratory muscles. Independent breathing may become impossible, necessitating lifelong artificial respiration. The paralyses can also lead to death."[145]

As Rotarians, we try to make a substantial contribution to PolioPlus:

> "PolioPlus" is the main humanitarian project of Rotary clubs around the world: the fight against polio (poliomyelitis, or polio for short).
>
> PolioPlus is an unparalleled success story: Since 1985, when Rotary International made the official decision to rid the world of this infectious disease, well over 99 percent of the task has been accomplished: At that time, there were still 125 countries with 350,000 new infections per year, but thanks to comprehensive vaccination measures, the

number of new infections per year has since been reduced to 140 (2020). Only in two countries - Afghanistan and Pakistan - is the population still acutely threatened by polio viruses.

Rotary did not achieve this success alone, but in cooperation with the World Health Organization (WHO), the children's relief organization UNICEF, and the U.S. health authority CDC. This Global Polio Eradication Initiative (GPEI), which also includes the GAVI vaccination alliance and, since 2009, the Bill & Melinda Gates Foundation as an additional partner, has been working since 1988 to permanently break the chain of infection - and is determined to achieve this goal. Polio will then be the second disease to disappear from the face of the earth, after smallpox."[146]

Donations for our RAAM polio eradication project came from Rotary clubs in Europe and the U.S., Rotary districts, many individuals, and businesses. The Rotary Fellowship Cycling to Serve supported us. We launched countless initiatives, gave many presentations and organized charity events. Christoph Strasser provided us with his jersey, which he had specially made for his 24-hour world record in 2021. We raffled it off among all those who donated to him as part of this campaign. All our donations were tripled by the Bill & Melinda Gates Foundation.

Our media team with Hubert, Martin and Roland had done a great job. We had a whole big stage: The sports channel K19 reported every day during the race. Martin Böckle got up at 5 a.m. every day during the race to finish the reports so that they would be online in Austria in time for breakfast. We had liveblogs in the Tiroler Tageszeitung, in the Rotary Magazin Online and in the Radsportnews, the ORF and Servus TV reported, we were in all the big Austrian newspapers. Martin Roseneder, who acted as my press spokesman, put in a lot of effort. Hundreds of thousands of people were able to follow us live every day! Christoph Strasser invited me to his podcast "Sitzfleisch" after the race. I gave numerous interviews and was even in Rennrad Magazine, a major German road cycling magazine. I hardly noticed any of the big media hype during the race. Back in Austria, I first became aware of the attention we had received. People I didn't even know kept talking to me about RAAM. During a lunch break, I once walked across the campus of my university. When I passed a larger group of students, they applauded spontaneously.

Since our first RAAM participation in 2016, we have raised over $4.2 million in donations to eradicate polio. We'll never know, but from a purely statistical standpoint, it's likely that we've been able to protect a few children from this terrible disease with the vaccinations our project has made possible. What more could we want to achieve? "We ride so that others can walk" - that is our mission.

A few weeks after RAAM, we received the Race Across America Lon Haldeman Award, which is given annually to the team that raises the most money for a charitable project. We had already received this award once in 2018 - now the second time in 2022.

The governor of our Rotary district, Heinz Rieder, invited me to a big Rotary event in Salzburg on September 17, 2022, to give a presentation about our Race Across America project. Afterwards he surprised me with the International Service Award for a Polio free world.

This award is given once a year to a maximum of ten Rotarians. The Rotary Magazine wrote about it:

"He challenges himself so that others don't get sick: Kurt Matzler cycles up to 5,000 km to raise funds for polio. Now he has been honored for this by Rotary International. The district had been keeping an eye on Kurt Matzler's commitment to the fight against polio for some time: at the Race Across America, which generates more than 1 million euros in donations each time, at bicycle races around Austria and across Italy, with polio promotion at his professionally motivated management talks, and so on. Now the achievement of the exceptional cyclist (by the way also Rotarian world champion with the over 45-year-olds) should be recognized. Walter Ebner (Pastgovernor D1920) did not miss the opportunity to deliver the award personally." [147]

What began in 2016 as an idea from Bob McKenzie has grown into an impressive international fundraising project. Today, over six years after our first RAAM as a team of four and pretty much six months after my solo participation, I still can't quite believe what we have achieved as a team.

Oceanside before the start: The team is almost complete - only Liane is missing (Photo: Hubert Siller)

RAAMbulance Car: Ruth Brandstätter, Alexandra Podpeskar, Liane Fendt (from left) (Photo: Martin Ebster)

RAAMCAM (Media-Car): Roland Volderauer, Hubert Siller, Martin Ebster (from left) (Photo: Ruth Brandstätter)

RAAMerica Car: Darlene McKenzie, Bill Clark, Bob McKenzie (from left) (Photo: Ruth Brandstätter)

RAAMbler Car: Zoltàn Bogdàn, Balàsz Vargas, Florian Phleps (from left) (Photo: Ruth Brandstätter)

Start in Oceanside, on June 14, 2022, 13:05 (Photo: Vic Armijo)

The first night in the desert (Photo: Vic Armijo)

Five minutes of relaxation after a night of riding (Photo: Florian Phleps)

Desperation on the 2nd race day: Big detour around Flagstaff and two broken bikes (Photo: Florian Phleps)

Sunrise in Monument Valley, at the bike rack of the media vehicle the broken bike (Photo: Florian Phleps)

Monument Valley (Photo: Florian Phleps)

Infinite vastness (Photo: Florian Phleps)

Ascent Wolf Creek Pass in the Rocky Mountains during rain (Photo: Hubert Siller)

Wind in the Great Plains (Photo: Florian Phleps)

Mississippi River - a milestone (Photo: Florian Phleps)

Shielded by the support vehicle in heavy traffic (Photo: Martin Ebster)

Knee pain (Photo: Hubert Siller)

Annapolis! (Photo: Florian Phleps)

The Race Across America Lon Haldeman Award for the highest fundraising number at RAAM 2022 (Photo: Kurt Matzler)

The sports channel K19 reported before, during and after the race. The videos can be found on YouTube. There were also extensive studio interviews before the race and after the race. You can find the links to them here (they are in German). After the race Florian Kraschitzer and Christoph Strasser invited me to their podcast "Sitzfleisch". You can also find the link to it here.

Studio talk before the Race Across America at K19 - together with Martin Ebster, Hubert Siller and Martin Böckle in March 2020. We talk about the preparations, the strategy and the challenges.

Studio talk after the Race Across America at K19 - together with Martin Ebster and Hubert Siller. We talk about our experiences, about our experiences and the crew.

Guest on "Sitzfleisch", the podcast by Florian Kraschitzer and Christoph Strasser.

TV recording of the 4GameChanger TV discussion by Puls24 "What can management learn from top-class sports?" with Patrick Ortlieb (Olympic champion, world champion, ÖSV finance officer and successful businessman), Ingeborg Freudenthaler (entrepreneur), Florian Grasel (ultra-rail runner) and Bastian Kaltenböck (former ski jumper and now winemaker in southern Styria), moderated by Martin Böckle.

I welcome feedback and comments on this book: kurt.matzler@uibk.ac.at

Literature

Amabile, T. M., Hadley, C. N., & Kramer, S. J. 2002. Creativity under the gun. *Harvard business review*, 80: 52-63.

Amabile, T. M., & Kramer, S. J. 2011. The power of small wins. *Harvard business review*, 89(5): 70-80.

Barker, E., & Wayne, R. 2017. *Barking up the wrong tree*: HarperCollins.

Barnes, C. M. 2018. Sleep well, lead better. *Harvard Business Review*(September-October): 2-5.

Barth, S. 2022. *Ultracycling & Bick Packing*: LongDistanceMedia.

Baumeister, R. F. 2015. Conquer yourself conquer the world. *Scientific American*, 312(4): 60-65.

Baumeister, R. F., & Tierney, J. 2012. *Willpower: Rediscovering the greatest human strength*: Penguin.

Behson, S. 2014. Work-Live Balance Through Interval Training. *Harvard Business Review*, Digital Article.

Berglund, B., & Berglund, L. 2015. Shermer's neck« is a rare injury in long-distance cycle races. Association with diplopia described for the first time, *Lakartidningen*, Vol. 112: DR7I.

Burns, L., Weissensteiner, J. R., & Cohen, M. 2019. Lifestyles and mindsets of Olympic, Paralympic and world champions: is an integrated approach the key to elite performance? *British Journal of Sports Medicine*, 53(13): 818-824.

Christensen, C., Allworth, J., & Dillen, K. 2012. *How will you measure your life*: Harper Collins.

Cialdini, R. 2001. Harnessing the science of persuasion. *Harvard Business Review*, 79(9): 72-79.

Cialdini, R. B. 2007. *Influence: The Psychology of Persuasion*. New York: Collins.

Clear, J. 2018. *Atomic Habits: An Easy and Proven Way to Build Good Habits and Break Bad Ones*: Avery.

Coleman, J. 2022. *HBR Guide to Crafting your Purpose*. Boston: Harvard Business Review Press.

Craig, N., & Snook, S. 2014. From purpose to impact. *Harvard business review*, 92(5): 104-111.

Czeisler, C. A., & Fryer, B. 2006. Sleep deficit: The performance killer. *Harvard Business Review*, 84(10): 53-59.

Czycholl, H. 2014. Müde Manager handeln, als wären sie betrunken. *Die Welt*(17. Jänner).

Dijksterhuis, A., & Meurs, T. 2006. Where creativity resides: The generative power of unconscious thought. *Consciousness and cognition*, 15(1): 135-146.

Dijksterhuis, A., & Nordgren, L. F. 2006. A theory of unconscious thought. *Perspectives on Psychological science*, 1(2): 95-109.

DiMaggio, P., & Powell, W. W. 1983. The iron cage revisited: Collective rationality and institutional isomorphism in organizational fields. *American sociological review*, 48(2): 147-160.

Drucker, P. F. 2004. What makes an effective executive. *Harvard business review*, 82(6): 17-21.

Elberse, A. 2022. Number One in Formula One. *Harvard Business Review*, 100(11-12): 70-78.

Evans, J. S. B., & Frankish, K. E. 2009. *In two minds: Dual processes and beyond*: Oxford University Press.

Fasching, W. 2015. *Die Kraft der Gedanken: ... und wie diese unser Leben prägen* Egoth Verlag.

Frankl, V. E. 1985. *Man's search for meaning*: Simon and Schuster.

Gladwell, M. 2013. *David and Goliath: Underdogs, Misfits and the Art of Battling Giants*. London: Penguin.

Gokulnath, S. 2021. *Let Go*. Las Vegas, USA.

Goleman, D. 2013. The focused leader. *Harvard business review*, 91(12): 50-60.

Grant, A. 2013. In the company of givers and takers. *Harvard Business Review*, 91(4): 90-97.

Grubinger, M., Gepp, M., & Gepp, A. 2010. ***Vom Traum zum Ziel: Alex Gepp beim Race Across America***: Egoth Verlag.

Gruebele, M., & Scott, G. 2017. ***Masters RAAM. A winning strategy***: Amazon Distribution GmbH.

Hedges, K. 2017. 5 Questons to Help Your Employees Find Their Inner Purpose. *Harvard Business Review*(Digital Article).

Hill, P. L., & Turiano, N. A. 2014. Purpose in life as a predictor of mortality across adulthood. ***Psychological science***, 25(7): 1482-1486.

Hinterhuber, H. H. 2015. ***Neue Zitate für Manager***: Frankfurter Allgemeine Buch.

Hughes, J., & Kehlenbach, D. 2011. ***Radsport Extrem: Die komplette Anleitung für Radmarathons, RTFs, Ultra- und Etappenrennen***: spomedis.

Jaklitsch, T. 2016. ***Coach dich selbst zu deinem besseren Ich!: Mentale Strategien von Race-Across-America-Rekordhalter Christoph Strasser***: Leykam.

Jobson, S., & Irvine, D. 2017. ***Ultra-Distance Cycling: An Expert Guide to Endurance Cycling***: Bloomsbury Publishing.

Kane, M., & Trochim, W. M. 2009. Concept mapping for applied social research. ***The Sage handbook of applied social research methods***: 435-474.

Keller, S., & Meaney, M. 2017. High-performing teams: A timeless leadership topic. ***McKinsey Quarterly***, 3(July): 81-87.

Koehn, N. F. 2010. Leadership in Crisis: Enest Shackleton and the Epic Voyage of the Endurance. ***Harvard Business School Case***(9-803-127).

Kunzmann, K. 2019. Schlaf, Cheflein, schlaf: Warum dauerhafter Schlafmangel für Körper und Gesit fatale Folgen hat. ***Die Absatzwirtschaft***(28. Januar).

Loehr, J., & Schwartz, T. 2001. The making of a corporate athlete. ***Harvard business review***, 79(1): 120-129.

Loehr, J., & Schwartz, T. 2003. *The power of full engagement. Managing energy, not time, is the key to high performance and personal renewal*: Simon and Schuster.

Löhr, G. 2018. *9 Tage 22 Stunden 40 Minuten: 4960 Kilometer nonstop beim härtesten Radrennen der Welt*: Mental Enterprises.

Magiera, C. 2009. *Einsatz und Anwendungen von Innovationstechnicken: Betrachtung unter dem Effizienzaspekt*: Diplomica Verlag.

Matzler, K., Stadler, C., Hautz, J., Friedrich von den Eichen, S., & Anschober, M. 2022. *Open Strategy: Durch offene Strategieprozesse Disruption erfolgreich meistern*. München: Vahlen Verlag.

McClean, S. T., Koopman, J., Yim, J., & Klotz, A. C. 2021. Stumbling out of the gate: The energy-based implications of morning routine disruption. *Personnel Psychology*, 74(3): 411-448.

Mickle, T. 2020. How Tim Cook Made Apple His Own. (7. August).

Milne, S., Orbell, S., & Sheeran, P. 2002. Combining motivational and volitional interventions to promote exercise participation: Protection motivation theory and implementation intentions. *British journal of health psychology*, 7(2): 163-184.

Misch, D. 2016. *Randonnée: Ein Ultra-Cycling Tagebuch*: Egoth Verlag.

Misch, D. 2021. *1000/24. Christoph Strasser und die Jagd nach dem perfekten Tag*: Covadonga Verlag.

Mischel, W., Shoda, Y., & Rodriguez, M. L. 1989. Delay of gratification in children. *Science*, 244(4907): 933-938.

N.N. 2018. The Psychology of Purpose: The John Templeton Foundation.

Nehls, M. 2012. *Herausforderung Race Across America: 4800 km Zeitfahren von Küste zu Küste*: Mental Enterprises.

Neumanr, G. 1999. Hitzebelastung und Hitzeakklimatisation im Sport. *Schweizerische Zeitschrift für Sportmedizin und Sporttraumatologie*, 47(2): 101-105.

Nyer, P. U., & Dellande, S. 2010. Public commitment as a motivator for weight loss. *Psychology & Marketing*, 27(1): 1-12.

Orbell, S., Hodgkins, S., & Sheeran, P. 1997. Implementation intentions and the theory of planned behavior. *Personality and social psychology bulletin*, 23(9): 945-954.

Pencavel, J. 2015. The productivity of working hours. *The Economic Journal*, 125(589): 2052-2076.

Porter, M. 1996. What is strategy? *Harvard Business Review*, 74(6): 61-78.

Porter, M. E., & Nohria, N. 2018. How CEOs manage time. *Harvard Business Review*, 96(4): 42-51.

Purps-Pardigol, S. 2021. *Leben mit Hirn: Wie Sie Ihre Potenziale entfalten, egal was um Sie herum geschieht.* : Campus Verlag.

Ranadivè, V. 2014. What a CEO Learned Coaching His Daughter's Basketball Team. *Entrepreneur* July 7.

Rees, J. 2021. *Vicious Cycle*. The EI Guru Publishing.

Reeves, M. 2017. *One long day*. CreateSpace Independent Publishing Platform.

Ritter, S. M., & Dijksterhuis, A. 2014. Creativity—the unconscious foundations of the incubation period. *Frontiers in human neuroscience*: 215.

Rosekind, M. R., Neri, D. F., Miller, D. L., Gregory, K. B., Webbon, L. L., & Oyung, R. L. 1997. Crew fatigue research focusing on development and use of effective countermeasures. *ICAO Journal*, 52(4): 20-22.

Simpson, N., Gibbs, E., & Matheson, G. 2017. Optimizing sleep to maximize performance: implications and recommendations for elite athletes. *Scandinavian journal of medicine & science in sports*, 27(3): 266-274.

Strasser, C. 2018. *Der Weg ist weiter als das Ziel*. Wien: egoth Verlag.

Stulberg, B., & Magness, S. 2017. *Peak performance: Elevate your game, avoid burnout, and thrive with the new science of success*: Rodale.

Thaler, R., & Sunstein, C. 2008. *Nudge: improving decisions about health, wealth and happiness* New Haven, CT: Yale University Press.

Traunmüller, K. 2011. *Am Limit. Race Across America*. Linz: Easy-Media Druck&Verlag.

Vallacher, R. R., & Wegner, D. M. 2014. *A theory of action identification*: Psychology Press.

Wansink, B. 2006. *Mindless eating: Why we eat more than we think*. New York: Bantam.

Wansink, B. 2008. *Essen ohne Sinn und Verstand: Wie die Lebensmittelindustrie uns manipuliert*: Campus Verlag.

Watson Peláez, M. 2011. Playn Your Way to Less Stress, More Happiness. *Time*, May, 31.

Weick, K. E. 1995. *Sensemaking in organizations*: Sage.

Williams, S. E., Cooley, S. J., Newell, E., Weibull, F., & Cumming, J. 2013. Seeing the difference: Developing effective imagery scripts for athletes. *Journal of Sport Psychology in Action*, 4(2): 109-121.

Williamson, A. M., & Feyer, A.-M. 2000. Moderate sleep deprivation produces impairments in cognitive and motor performance equivalent to legally prescribed levels of alcohol intoxication. *Occupational and environmental medicine*, 57(10): 649-655.

Wilson James, Q., & Kelling George, L. 1982. Broken Windows: The police and neighborhood safety. *The Atlantic*(March): 29-38.

Zimbardo, P. G. 1969. *The human choice: Individuation, reason, and order versus deindividuation, impulse, and chaos*. Paper presented at the Nebraska symposium on motivation.

Endnotes

[1] https://de.statista.com/infografik/24929/geschaetzte-anzahl-der-erfolgreichen-besteigungen-des-mt-everest/

[2] "Harder than climbing Mount Everest", Neue Züricher Zeitung, 03.07.2005

[3] https://commons.wikimedia.org/wiki/File:Blank_US_Map_With_Labels.svg; route line added

[4] Nehls, M. 2012. *Herausforderung Race Across America: 4800 km Zeitfahren von Küste zu Küste*: Mental Enterprises.

[5] https://www.racearoundaustria.at, Reprinted with permission

[6] Nehls, M. 2012. *Herausforderung Race Across America: 4800 km Zeitfahren von Küste zu Küste*: Mental Enterprises.

[7] Gruebele, M., & Scott, G. 2017. *Masters RAAM. A winning strategy*: Amazon Distribution GmbH.

[8] Nehls, M. 2012. *Herausforderung Race Across America: 4800 km Zeitfahren von Küste zu Küste*: Mental Enterprises.

[9] Strasser, C. 2018. *Der Weg ist weiter als das Ziel*. Wien: egoth Verlag.

[10] Löhr, G. 2018. *9 Tage 22 Stunden 40 Minuten: 4960 Kilometer nonstop beim härtesten Radrennen der Welt*: Mental Enterprises.

[11] Misch, D. 2016. *Randonnée: Ein Ultra-Cycling Tagebuch*: Egoth Verlag.

[12] Gruebele, M., & Scott, G. 2017. *Masters RAAM. A winning strategy*: Amazon Distribution GmbH.

[13] Grubinger, M., Gepp, M., & Gepp, A. 2010. *Vom Traum zum Ziel: Alex Gepp beim Race Across America*: Egoth Verlag.

[14] Gokulnath, S. 2021. *Let Go*. Las Vegas, USA.

[15] Traunmüller, K. 2011. *Am Limit. Race Across America*. Linz: Easy-Media Druck&Verlag.

[16] Reeves, M. 2017. *One long day*: CreateSpace Independent Publishing Platform.

[17] Rees, J. 2021. *Vicious Cycle*: The EI Guru Publishing.

[18] Jaklitsch, T. 2016. *Coach dich selbst zu deinem besseren Ich!: Mentale Strategien von Race-Across-America-Rekordhalter Christoph Strasser*: Leykam.

[19] Fasching, W. 2015. *Die Kraft der Gedanken: ... und wie diese unser Leben prägen* Egoth Verlag.

[20] Hughes, J., & Kehlenbach, D. 2011. *Radsport Extrem: Die komplette Anleitung für Radmarathons, RTFs, Ultra- und Etappenrennen*: spomedis.

[21] Jobson, S., & Irvine, D. 2017. *Ultra-Distance Cycling: An Expert Guide to Endurance Cycling*. Bloomsbury Publishing.

[22] Nehls, M. 2012. *Herausforderung Race Across America: 4800 km Zeitfahren von Küste zu Küste*. Mental Enterprises.

[23] Christensen, C., Allworth, J., & Dillen, K. 2012. *How will you measure your life*. Harper Collins.

[24] Baumeister, R. F. 2015. Conquer yourself conquer the world. *Scientific American*, 312(4): 60-65.

[25] Goleman, D. 2013. The focused leader. *Harvard business review*, 91(12): 50-60.

[26] Mischel, W., Shoda, Y., & Rodriguez, M. L. 1989. Delay of gratification in children. *Science*, 244(4907): 933-938.

[27] Baumeister, R. F., & Tierney, J. 2012. *Willpower: Rediscovering the greatest human strength*. Penguin.

[28] Baumeister, R. F. 2015. Conquer yourself conquer the world. *Scientific American*, 312(4): 60-65.

[29] Baumeister, R. F., & Tierney, J. 2012. *Willpower: Rediscovering the greatest human strength*. Penguin.

[30] Baumeister, R. F., & Tierney, J. 2012. *Willpower: Rediscovering the greatest human strength*. Penguin.

[31] Baumeister, R. F., & Tierney, J. 2012. *Willpower: Rediscovering the greatest human strength*. Penguin.

[32] Baumeister, R. F., & Tierney, J. 2012. *Willpower: Rediscovering the greatest human strength*. Penguin.

[33] Wansink, B. 2008. *Essen ohne Sinn und Verstand: Wie die Lebensmittelindustrie uns manipuliert*. Campus Verlag.

[34] Orbell, S., Hodgkins, S., & Sheeran, P. 1997. Implementation intentions and the theory of planned behavior. *Personality and social psychology bulletin*, 23(9): 945-954.

[35] Milne, S., Orbell, S., & Sheeran, P. 2002. Combining motivational and volitional interventions to promote exercise participation: Protection motivation theory and implementation intentions. *British journal of health psychology*, 7(2): 163-184.

[36] Cialdini, R. 2001. Harnessing the science of persuasion. *Harvard Business Review*, 79(9): 72-79.

[37] Cialdini, R. B. 2007. *Influence: The Psychology of Persuasion*. New York: Collins.

[38] Nyer, P. U., & Dellande, S. 2010. Public commitment as a motivator for weight loss. *Psychology & Marketing*, 27(1): 1-12.

[39] Baumeister, R. F., & Tierney, J. 2012. **Willpower: Rediscovering the greatest human strength**: Penguin.

[40] https://www.inc.com/melissa-chu/winston-churchills-lazy-strategy-to-getting-more-work-done.html

[41] McClean, S. T., Koopman, J., Yim, J., & Klotz, A. C. 2021. Stumbling out of the gate: The energy-based implications of morning routine disruption. **Personnel Psychology**, 74(3): 411-448.

[42] https://harpersbazaar.com.au/jennifer-aniston-morning-routine/

[43] McClean, S. T., Koopman, J., Yim, J., & Klotz, A. C. 2021. Stumbling out of the gate: The energy-based implications of morning routine disruption. **Personnel Psychology**, 74(3): 411-448.

[44] Clear, J. 2018. **Atomic Habits: An Easy and Proven Way to Build Good Habits and Break Bad Ones**: Avery.

[45] Hinterhuber, H. H. 2015. **Neue Zitate für Manager**: Frankfurter Allgemeine Buch.

[46] Neumanr, G. 1999. Hitzebelastung und Hitzeakklimatisation im Sport. **Schweizerische Zeitschrift für Sportmedizin und Sporttraumatologie**, 47(2): 101-105.

[47] Strasser, C. 2018. **Der Weg ist weiter als das Ziel**. Wien: egoth Verlag.

[48] Nehls, M. 2012. **Herausforderung Race Across America: 4800 km Zeitfahren von Küste zu Küste**: Mental Enterprises.

[49] Weick, K. E. 1995. **Sensemaking in organizations**: Sage.

[50] Kane, M., & Trochim, W. M. 2009. Concept mapping for applied social research. **The Sage handbook of applied social research methods**: 435-474.

[51] Drucker, P. F. 2004. What makes an effective executive. **Harvard business review**, 82(6): 17-21.

[52] Watson Pelàez, M. 2011. Playn Your Way to Less Stress, More Happiness. **Time**, May, 31.

[53] Barker, E., & Wayne, R. 2017. **Barking up the wrong tree**: HarperCollins.

[54] Frankl, V. E. 1985. **Man's search for meaning**: Simon and Schuster.

[55] Frankl, V. E. 1985. **Man's search for meaning**: Simon and Schuster.

[56] https://www.realtimeperformance.com/5-lessons-from-viktor-frankls-book-mans-search-for-meaning/

[57] Frankl, V. E. 1985. **Man's search for meaning**: Simon and Schuster.

[58] See for this Stulberg, B., & Magness, S. 2017. **Peak performance: Elevate your game, avoid burnout, and thrive with the new science of success**: Rodale.

[59] Stulberg, B., & Magness, S. 2017. *Peak performance: Elevate your game, avoid burnout, and thrive with the new science of success*. Rodale.

[60] Stulberg, B., & Magness, S. 2017. *Peak performance: Elevate your game, avoid burnout, and thrive with the new science of success*. Rodale.

[61] Coleman, J. 2022. *HBR Guide to Crafting your Purpose*. Boston: Harvard Business Review Press.

[62] https://www.gallup.com/education/248222/gallup-bates-purposeful-work-2019.aspx

[63] Craig, N., & Snook, S. 2014. From purpose to impact. *Harvard business review*, 92(5): 104-111.

[64] N.N. 2018. The Psychology of Purpose: The John Templeton Foundation. Hill, P. L., & Turiano, N. A. 2014. Purpose in life as a predictor of mortality across adulthood. *Psychological science*, 25(7): 1482-1486.

[65] Coleman, J. 2022. *HBR Guide to Crafting your Purpose*. Boston: Harvard Business Review Press.

[66] Coleman, J. 2022. *HBR Guide to Crafting your Purpose*. Boston: Harvard Business Review Press.

[67] Adapted from Coleman, J. 2022. *HBR Guide to Crafting your Purpose*. Boston: Harvard Business Review Press.

[68] Coleman, J. 2022. *HBR Guide to Crafting your Purpose*. Boston: Harvard Business Review Press.

[69] Grant, A. 2013. In the company of givers and takers. *Harvard Business Review*, 91(4): 90-97.

[70] Vallacher, R. R., & Wegner, D. M. 2014. *A theory of action identification*. Psychology Press.

[71] https://www.colegio-humboldt.edu.pe/refo/refo-2008/Materialien/08-2008%20Materialien/03%20Die%20Geschichte%20von%20den%20drei%20Steinmetzen.pdf

[72] Hedges, K. 2017. 5 Questons to Help Your Employees Find Their Inner Purpose. *Harvard Business Review* (Digital Article).

[73] Williams, S. E., Cooley, S. J., Newell, E., Weibull, F., & Cumming, J. 2013. Seeing the difference: Developing effective imagery scripts for athletes. *Journal of Sport Psychology in Action*, 4(2): 109-121.

[74] Burns, L., Weissensteiner, J. R., & Cohen, M. 2019. Lifestyles and mindsets of Olympic, Paralympic and world champions: is an integrated approach the key to elite performance? *British Journal of Sports Medicine*, 53(13): 818-824.

[75] https://www.169k.net/blog/straps-raam

[76] https://www.peaksports.com/sports-psychology-blog/sports-visualization-athletes/

[77] Amabile, T. M., & Kramer, S. J. 2011. The power of small wins. *Harvard business review*, 89(5): 70-80.

[78] Purps-Pardigol, S. 2021. *Leben mit Hirn: Wie Sie Ihre Potenziale entfalten, egal was um Sie herum geschieht.* : Campus Verlag.

[79] Crum, A. J., & Crum, T. (2015). Stress can be a good thing if you know how to use it. Harvard Business Review. Retrieved from https://hbr.org/2015/09/stress-can-be-a-good-thing-if-you-know-how-to-use-it.

[80] Rosekind, M. R., Neri, D. F., Miller, D. L., Gregory, K. B., Webbon, L. L., & Oyung, R. L. 1997. Crew fatigue research focusing on development and use of effective countermeasures. *ICAO Journal*, 52(4): 20-22.

[81] Berglund, B., & Berglund, L. 2015. Shermer's neck« is a rare injury in long-distance cycle races. Association with diplopia described for the first time, *Lakartidningen*, Vol. 112: DR7I.

[82] Barth, S. 2022. *Ultracycling & Bick Packing*: LongDistanceMedia.

[83] Barth, S. 2022. *Ultracycling & Bick Packing*: LongDistanceMedia.

[84] https://navyseals.com/nsw/hell-week-0/

[85] See in this regard. Barth, S. 2022. *Ultracycling & Bick Packing*: LongDistanceMedia.

[86] https://gannikus.de/medizin/was-ist-riechsalz-und-wie-effektiv-ist-es-auf-die-kraft/

[87] Grubinger, M., Gepp, M., & Gepp, A. 2010. *Vom Traum zum Ziel: Alex Gepp beim Race Across America*: Egoth Verlag.

[88] Porter, M. 1996. What is strategy? *Harvard Business Review*, 74(6): 61-78.

[89] DiMaggio, P., & Powell, W. W. 1983. The iron cage revisited: Collective rationality and institutional isomorphism in organizational fields. *American sociological review*, 48(2): 147-160.

[90] Matzler, K., Stadler, C., Hautz, J., Friedrich von den Eichen, S., & Anschober, M. 2022. *Open Strategy: Durch offene Strategieprozesse Disruption erfolgreich meistern*. München: Vahlen Verlag.

[91] Wansink, B. 2006. *Mindless eating: Why we eat more than we think*. New York: Bantam.

[92] Thaler, R., & Sunstein, C. 2008. *Nudge: improving decisions about health, wealth and happiness* New Haven, CT: Yale University Press.

[93] Thaler, R., & Sunstein, C. 2008. *Nudge: improving decisions about health, wealth and happiness* New Haven, CT: Yale University Press.

[94] Matzler, K., Stadler, C., Hautz, J., Friedrich von den Eichen, S., & Anschober, M. 2022. *Open Strategy: Durch offene Strategieprozesse Disruption erfolgreich meistern*. München: Vahlen Verlag.

[95] DiMaggio, P., & Powell, W. W. 1983. The iron cage revisited: Collective rationality and institutional isomorphism in organizational fields. *American sociological review*, 48(2): 147-160.

[96] Gladwell, M. 2013. *David and Goliath: Underdogs, Misfits and the Art of Battling Giants*. London: Penguin.

[97] Matzler, K., Stadler, C., Hautz, J., Friedrich von den Eichen, S., & Anschober, M. 2022. *Open Strategy: Durch offene Strategieprozesse Disruption erfolgreich meistern*. München: Vahlen Verlag.

[98] Ranadivè, V. 2014. What a CEO Learned Coaching His Daughter's Basketball Team. *Entrepreneur* July 7.

[99] Ranadivè, V. 2014. What a CEO Learned Coaching His Daughter's Basketball Team. *Entrepreneur* July 7.

[100] Wilson James, Q., & Kelling George, L. 1982. Broken Windows: The police and neighborhood safety. *The Atlantic*(March): 29-38, Zimbardo, P. G. 1969. *The human choice: Individuation, reason, and order versus deindividuation, impulse, and chaos*. Paper presented at the Nebraska symposium on motivation.

[101] Wilson James, Q., & Kelling George, L. 1982. Broken Windows: The police and neighborhood safety. *The Atlantic*(March): 29-38.

[102] Clear, J. 2018. *Atomic Habits: An Easy and Proven Way to Build Good Habits and Break Bad Ones*: Avery.

[103] Clear, J. 2018. *Atomic Habits: An Easy and Proven Way to Build Good Habits and Break Bad Ones*: Avery.

[104] https://www.bbc.com/sport/olympics/19174302

[105] https://www.christophstrasser.at/aktuelles_live_newsletter/news/aktuelles_detailansicht/mein-erstes-fazit-1day1000k/

[106] Misch, D. 2021. *1000/24. Christoph Strasser und die Jagd nach dem perfekten Tag*: Covadonga Verlag.

[107] https://pedalchile.com/blog/shaved-arms

[108] https://www.hilite-bikes.com/de/blog/post/wieviel-watt-ersparnis-bringt-eine-saubere-kette/

[109] Elberse, A. 2022. Number One in Formula One. *Harvard Business Review*, 100(11-12): 70-78.

[110] https://www.raceacrossamerica.org/resources/historic/EverythingByShermer.pdf

[111] Elberse, A. 2022. Number One in Formula One. *Harvard Business Review*, 100(11-12): 70-78.

[112] Keller, S., & Meaney, M. 2017. High-performing teams: A timeless leadership topic. *McKinsey Quarterly,* 3(July): 81-87.

[113] Keller, S., & Meaney, M. 2017. High-performing teams: A timeless leadership topic. *McKinsey Quarterly,* 3(July): 81-87.

[114] This advertisement is repeatedly reported in the literature, although it is unclear when and where it is said to have appeared, cf. Koehn, N. F. 2010. Leadership in Crisis: Enest Shackleton and the Epic Voyage of the Endurance. *Harvard Business School Case*(9-803-127).

[115] https://shackleton.com/en-at/blogs/articles/why-ernest-shackleton-is-still-relevant-today

[116] Source: https://de.statista.com/statistik/daten/studie/205260/umfrage/arbeitszeit-pro-woche-von-geschaeftsfuehrern/

[117] https://www.max-grundig-klinik.de/wp-content/uploads/max-grundig-klinik-presseinformation-04042016-schlaf.pdf

[118] https://www.max-grundig-klinik.de/wp-content/uploads/max-grundig-klinik-presseinformation-04042016-schlaf.pdf

[119] Porter, M. E., & Nohria, N. 2018. How CEOs manage time. *Harvard Business Review*, 96(4): 42-51.

[120] Kunzmann, K. 2019. Schlaf, Cheflein, schlaf: Warum dauerhafter Schlafmangel für Körper und Gesit fatale Folgen hat. *Die Absatzwirtschaft*(28. Januar).

[121] Mickle, T. 2020. How Tim Cook Made Apple His Own. (7. August).

[122] https://www.cnbc.com/2018/11/05/elon-musk-on-working-120-hours-a-week-youll-go-bonkers.html

[123] Barnes, C. M. 2018. Sleep well, lead better. *Harvard Business Review*(September-October): 2-5.

[124] Czycholl, H. 2014. Müde Manager handeln, als wären sie betrunken. *Die Welt*(17. Jänner).

[125] Loehr, J., & Schwartz, T. 2003. *The power of full engagement. Managing energy, not time, is the key to high performance and personal renewal*: Simon and Schuster.

[126] Loehr, J., & Schwartz, T. 2001. The making of a corporate athlete. *Harvard business review*, 79(1): 120-129.

[127] Loehr, J., & Schwartz, T. 2001. The making of a corporate athlete. *Harvard business review*, 79(1): 120-129.

[128] Stulberg, B., & Magness, S. 2017. *Peak performance: Elevate your game, avoid burnout, and thrive with the new science of success*: Rodale.

[129] Pencavel, J. 2015. The productivity of working hours. *The Economic Journal*, 125(589): 2052-2076.

[130] Amabile, T. M., Hadley, C. N., & Kramer, S. J. 2002. Creativity under the gun. *Harvard business review*, 80: 52-63.

[131] Magiera, C. 2009. *Einsatz und Anwendungen von Innovationstechnicken: Betrachtung unter dem Effizienzaspekt*: Diplomica Verlag.

[132] Evans, J. S. B., & Frankish, K. E. 2009. *In two minds: Dual processes and beyond*: Oxford University Press.

[133] Dijksterhuis, A., & Nordgren, L. F. 2006. A theory of unconscious thought. *Perspectives on Psychological science*, 1(2): 95-109.

[134] Ritter, S. M., & Dijksterhuis, A. 2014. Creativity—the unconscious foundations of the incubation period. *Frontiers in human neuroscience*: 215.

[135] Dijksterhuis, A., & Meurs, T. 2006. Where creativity resides: The generative power of unconscious thought. *Consciousness and cognition*, 15(1): 135-146.

[136] Stulberg, B., & Magness, S. 2017. *Peak performance: Elevate your game, avoid burnout, and thrive with the new science of success*: Rodale.

[137] Loehr, J., & Schwartz, T. 2001. The making of a corporate athlete. *Harvard business review*, 79(1): 120-129.

[138] Simpson, N., Gibbs, E., & Matheson, G. 2017. Optimizing sleep to maximize performance: implications and recommendations for elite athletes. *Scandinavian journal of medicine & science in sports*, 27(3): 266-274.

[139] Czeisler, C. A., & Fryer, B. 2006. Sleep deficit: The performance killer. *Harvard Business Review*, 84(10): 53-59.

[140] Barnes, C. M. 2018. Sleep well, lead better. *Harvard Business Review*(September-October): 2-5.

[141] Czeisler, C. A., & Fryer, B. 2006. Sleep deficit: The performance killer. *Harvard Business Review*, 84(10): 53-59.

[142] Williamson, A. M., & Feyer, A.-M. 2000. Moderate sleep deprivation produces impairments in cognitive and motor performance equivalent to legally prescribed levels of alcohol intoxication. *Occupational and environmental medicine*, 57(10): 649-655.

[143] Loehr, J., & Schwartz, T. 2001. The making of a corporate athlete. *Harvard business review*, 79(1): 120-129.

[144] Behson, S. 2014. Work-Live Balance Through Interval Training. *Harvard Business Review*, Digital Article.

[145] https://www.sozialministerium.at/Themen/Gesundheit/Uebertragbare-Krankheiten/Infektionskrankheiten-A-Z/Kinderl%C3%A4hmung-(poliomyelitis).html

[146] https://rotary.de/endpolionow/

[147] https://rotary.de/gesundheit/service-award-fuer-kurt-matzler-a-20741.html

Printed in Great Britain
by Amazon